YOUR Destiny TAKEN BY FORCE

NO MORE EXCUSES

Trina,
Thank you for your support awesome woman of God!
God bless you

YOUR *Destiny* TAKEN BY FORCE
NO MORE EXCUSES

MONIQUE M. BECK

REDEMPTION PRESS

© 2017 by Monique Beck. All rights reserved.

Published by Redemption Press, PO Box 427, Enumclaw, WA 98022

Toll Free (844) 2REDEEM (273-3336)

Redemption Press is honored to present this title in partnership with the author. The views expressed or implied in this work are those of the author. Redemption Press provides our imprint seal representing design excellence, creative content, and high quality production.

No part of this publication may be reproduced, stored in a retrieval system, or transmitted in any way by any means—electronic, mechanical, photocopy, recording, or otherwise—without the prior permission of the copyright holder, except as provided by USA copyright law.

All Scripture quotations, unless otherwise indicated, are taken from the Holy Bible, King James Version, © 1979, 1980, 1982 by Thomas Nelson, Inc., Publishers. Used by permission.

ISBN 13: 978-1-68314-167-9 (Print)

978-1-68314-168-6 (ePub)

978-1-68314-169-3 (Mobi)

Library of Congress Catalog Card Number: 2017932290

This book is dedicated to the advancement of the kingdom of God. I pray that it encourages, inspires, invigorates, and mobilizes you to pursue your purpose.

In Jesus' name, Amen.

Contents

Preface: Believe in the Greater in You ix
Introduction: Tapping into Destiny xiii
1 – Proclaiming, Decreeing, and Declaring 17
2 – Confessing, Revealing, and Facing 27
3 – Understanding, Searching Out, and Seeking God 39
4 – Understanding Acceptance 51
5 – Forgiveness 59
6 – Restoration and Revitalization 67
7 – Provision 75
8 – Producing 81
9 – Manifestation 93
Sources 101

Preface

BELIEVE IN THE GREATER IN YOU

My inspiration for this book came directly from God during a fast that He called me to do in November of 2015. It was to be 105 days of self-examination. During this time of abstaining (food consisted of mostly fruits, vegetables, nuts, berries and whole grains), there were many things God showed me as He began to pour. The person I was pretending to be was not in tune with the person God said I was. I had become very complacent, my eating was out of control, and my mind would just run in 1,000 directions. I couldn't even pray without thinking about some care of the world, as the Bible talks about. I had fallen away from my first love, Christ, and I needed to be refreshed, restored, and revived.

During my time of abstaining, God showed me myself in a way I had never seen before. As He helped me through my process, He called me to write down what He stirred within me. I did not know how it would be humanly possible to complete the task He presented, but His strength was made perfect in my weakness. As I submitted to God in obedience, He was faithful in delivering me from my number one hindrance—self-condemnation.

It's amazing that we can often see other people on a higher plane and in a greater place, but it is sometimes challenging to see ourselves in that same place. Not that we should covet someone else's blessings, but rather that we should pursue the great God who resides in us. Jesus said greater works shall we do on earth than He did, but we cannot achieve those works without first having the belief that we can.

At the end of the 105 days, I completed the fast, completed this book's first draft a few days later, and had a new take on life! God is good, and He will never give us a task that we are not able to complete. He has a divine plan and purpose for His people, but we must first be willing to accept the challenge. Because God allowed me to take my destiny by force, He has inspired me to write about how others can do the same.

Acknowledgments

I would like to give special thanks to:
- My Lord and Savior Jesus Christ for entrusting me with a word to deliver to Your people. I love You!
- My best friend and husband, Ray, for loving, supporting, encouraging, and sticking with me through thick and thin in my pursuit of destiny. Thank you for understanding that my staying up countless nights to work on this assignment was necessary. I love and appreciate you, honey!
- My children for holding me accountable and asking me every so often how the book was coming along. I love you!
- My mother, father, and family members who have prayed for me since I was a child and continuously. Thank you for training me up in the way that I should go. I love you!
- Apostle and Prophetess Vaughn of Fit for the Kingdom Ministries and Christian Education Center for delivering an uncut, life-changing word. Thank you for speaking into my life and challenging me to pursue my purpose. I love you!

- Sister Aikens for reading my first draft. Thank you for your feedback!
- Dr. Juanita Bynum for bringing an encouraging word via @3WithME on Facebook. Thank you for your obedience. Love you!
- My sisters in Christ who rooted me on over the years! Love you ladies!
- The men and women of God who have spoken into my life and prophesied over the years. Thank you for your obedience.

Introduction

TAPPING INTO DESTINY

Imagine yourself running a race, and you are taking it one step at a time. You encounter many struggles along the way. Your eyes begin to burn profusely as the sweat seeps down on your eyelashes. Your shoes come untied and you need to stop and lace them back up. The heat from the sun is relentless, as it seeks to warm up everything in its path. You hear your friends rooting for you and your enemies booing you. You're tired, thirsty, hungry, and you so badly want to just take a break and relax. As all of these thoughts run through your head, your feet are still moving and are crossing the finish line.

You have no idea how you made it over and are overcome with emotion. You begin to think about how badly you wanted to quit and what would have happened if you did. You reflect on your darkest times of the race, when you envied the ones who passed you up along the way. You look around and you wonder if they made it and how they were able to make it if they did. After all, you hadn't trained like they had. They had weeks, months, and maybe even years to prepare when you only had what seemed to be days. After all, you were out of shape, you didn't know the difference between the starting line and the finish line, and had no idea how you would finish the course.

As you continue to reflect on what you thought you could not do, you are humbled as you realize that you are right! You could not have made it without that flicker of hope, that feeling of victory, and that Cheerleader living and breathing in you. Yes! It was because of Jesus that you were able to take part in the celebration. It was because of His strength that was made perfect in your weakness that you were able to see the manifestation of what you had envisioned.

You shed tears of joy and are overcome with happiness. As you look around and don't see all the people with whom you started, you wonder what happened. You were so sure that all the super-athletic runners would make it, while you questioned the slow starters' (including yourself) longevity. What you find, however, is that the group who endured to the end of the race was not whom you assumed it would be. Suddenly, you realize the significance of the scripture that says, "Let us run with patience the race that is set before us. Looking unto Jesus the author and finisher of our faith" (Heb. 12:1-2).

You are victorious, you are an overcomer, and now you know that you really can do all things through Christ who strengthens you! You never envisioned how wonderful the celebration would be, as you are in awe of His faithfulness. This time, you didn't let anything stop you, and you are so glad you kept going! You realized that you really are great, just like God said you were!

Who doesn't want to be victorious and accomplish the "race" set before them? Who doesn't want to be a part of the winner's circle, knowing they have endured every trial and tribulation and never gave up? Well, I have to tell you that there was a time in my life when I could not see myself winning. Those who actually win do what is required to win, whereas others don't. They visualize themselves in a greater place, and they strive and fight to get there. They realize that the work won't do itself, and despite how they feel, they have to keep moving.

One of the main obstacles I have had to overcome was my weight loss. I wanted to lose weight for years, and I went through a vicious cycle of losing and gaining. I would sign up for a weight loss program, lose ten to fifteen pounds, and the weight would just come right back when I *stopped* doing what was required to sustain the loss. I got so caught up in the victory of the short-term goal that I lost sight of the long-term goal. Other times I would plateau and immediately get discouraged and give up on it.

At the age of 29, my weight peaked to an all-time high of 279 lbs. At 5'-11" tall, 279 lbs. can be masked for a little while, but it cannot be hidden forever. People would say things like, "You are big-boned" or "You wouldn't look right if you lost a bunch of weight." Meanwhile, I was dying on the inside. I was always tired, I could not walk up a flight of stairs without losing my breath, and I was very uncomfortable in my own skin. I had wallowed in my depression of disappointing weight loss long enough, and I needed to make a change. I knew that it would not be easy, but I realized I needed to be patient with myself and the process.

Before I could even begin to tap into my destiny, I had to envision myself beyond where I was at the time. I had to believe that forward movement in the right direction would eventually equal success. I had to come into agreement with the plans God has for my life and, most importantly—I had to be alive to accomplish them. When my doctor wanted to put me on high cholesterol medication at the age of about 31, I knew I needed to do something different. It's impossible to tap into destiny without a pulse, and I was definitely headed in that direction.

So what does it take to get to the above beautiful scene of the runner who accomplished his race? Things always seem easier said than done, but in life. we can never count anyone out (including ourselves). Envision yourself being greater than you are today. God sees you as the wonderful, miraculous, beautifully amazing person He placed in your mother's womb.

You *can* run this race and you *can* fight this fight through the power of God working within you. Regardless of where you find yourself in life at this moment, God sees you as far greater. God loves you and because of His love, He laid down His life to give you one. God wants you to walk out the destiny and purpose He designed for you, but you must be willing to take accountability for what that means. Everyone's walk will be different, but it is up to each individual to tap into his/her own purpose.

What will you do to take full advantage of the opportunity that stands before you in this race called life? What will your diet need to entail so that you are healthy enough to run well? What types of vitamins will you need to take to get all the nutrients your body requires? Will you suffer from dehydration along the way, or will you stay hydrated with the living water? There will most definitely be obstacles along the way, but will you be one of them?

This book is designed to help you get on track, stay on track, and pursue the will of God for your life. God wants to use you mightily, and He wants you to live in abundance. Ask God for a fresh pair of sneakers if you need them, lace them up, and let's get to work! Time is of the essence, and we only have until the sun goes down on our marathons. Destiny awaits!

Chapter 1
PROCLAIMING, DECREEING, AND DECLARING

While writing this book, some of the sisters at my church and I did a fast and a shut-in. A shut-in, as defined by our church, is a time when people gather together in one accord in prayer, thanksgiving, worship, supplication, and intercession to God on behalf of others. The "shut-in" part took place when we locked and covered the door for a period of 12 hours straight. To say that this intimate time with God changed my life is an understatement.

To pray is one thing, but to pray with belief is another. During our prayer meeting, each person would take turns praying about a specific area of ministry, the world, families, etc. When I knew that it was close to my time to pray, I would get knots in my stomach and feel complete inadequacy. It wasn't because I had never believed in the effectiveness of fervent prayer, but I personally knew that my relationship with God was lacking at the time. I wondered why God would ever want to hear from me, being that it was becoming more of a daily routine for me not to pray. I was angry, depressed, and disappointed. Nothing seemed to be changing in my life, and I was tired of it. I was merely existing and not living my best life.

As I began to open my mouth and asked God to forgive me—I reconnected with Him. Immediately, I felt a weight lifted. The power of God fell on me as I ministered His Word back to Him. I was reminded through the Scriptures of the greater God living within me and that there is power in the name of Jesus. I sensed the shifting taking place in my spirit, as God was transitioning me into a place of purpose and out of the mindset of mess.

God knew I had lost sight of my purpose, ultimately my destiny, and He was not having it! As I prayed, I thought about how God never gave up on me and how He loved me. I was convicted when I thought about how I had lost sight of His plan and how precious His Word is. I was empowered when I began to repeat the good thoughts that God has for me, according to what is recorded in His Word. Realizing the power of life and death residing in my tongue, I prayed with confidence. I declared that I would live a life without fear or self-condemnation for the rest of my days.

Proclaiming

Have you ever heard the saying, "A closed mouth doesn't get fed"? Well in biblical times, people didn't just expect things to happen in life (what some consider fate), but they took possession of what God said they could have. They had both faith and understanding in a God who could do anything but fail. Even the recorded proclamations by God Himself were very specific and their intended purpose was assured. God's desire is that in these times, we would be strategic in our proclamations to Him as well. He doesn't want us to just get whatever we get, but rather what He predestined us to have. Through biblical examples, we see that people proclaimed the Word of God, called out the Word of God, cried out and spared not. They had some power behind what they released into the earth, as they had a blessed assurance that it would surely come to pass.

Proclaiming, Decreeing, and Declaring

In the book of Exodus, Moses asked God to show him His glory, and the Lord said that no man has ever seen the face of God and lived. God did, however, make a way for Moses to experience His glory without him being consumed in the process. In essence, Moses got what he asked for and God was glorified in the process.

> And he said, I will make all my goodness pass before thee, and I will proclaim the name of the LORD before thee; and will be gracious to whom I will be gracious, and will shew mercy on whom I will shew mercy. And he said, Thou canst not see my face: for there shall no man see me, and live. (Ex. 33:19-20)

Please read Exodus 34:1-10. Moses went up to Mt. Sinai alone to commune with God for 40 days to get instruction for the people of God. It was at that time that the Lord descended in the cloud, stood with him there, and proclaimed the name of the Lord. Yes, the Lord proclaimed His own name. If the Lord proclaims His own name, how much more should we do so on earth. We must know who we are and Whose we are so we are sure that we are headed in the right direction. We cannot begin to take our destinies by force without having a clear direction or perception for what we ought to do. One thing we can do today, however, is declare that we are God's beloved! Prayerfully discover God's purpose so you can write the vision and make it plain in your life.

> And the LORD passed by before him, and proclaimed, The LORD, the LORD God merciful and gracious, longsuffering, and abundant in goodness and truth, keeping mercy for thousands, forgiving iniquity and transgression and sin, and that will by no means clear the guilty; visiting the iniquity of the fathers upon the children, and upon the children's children, unto the third and to the fourth generation. (Ex. 34:6-7)

Please read Isaiah 62 and capture this highlight from the chapter:

Behold, the LORD hath proclaimed unto the end of the world, Say ye to the daughter of Zion, Behold, thy salvation cometh; behold, his reward is with him, and his work before him. And they shall call them, The holy people, The redeemed of the LORD: and thou shalt be called, Sought out, A city not forsaken. (Isa. 62:11-12)

We are the "sought out" and we are not forsaken! God is here and has always been here. He is very serious about His children, and His desire is that none be sifted as wheat as Luke 22 explains. We are God's chosen, and He wants to use us for His glory. You may not believe that now, but you will by the time you get finished reading this book. I decree and declare that your life will never be the same in the name of Jesus! God will operate through you and in you until the day of Jesus Christ.

During this time of fellowship with the Lord, allow God to show you the specific purpose for which He placed you on earth. Only you can take your destiny by force. You were custom-made to walk the path God has prepared, and no one can do it quite like you. Destiny is like Cinderella's slipper. The slipper would only fit her foot and no one else's. The question about your destiny is whether or not it will be taken out of the box and tried on for size.

Let me encourage you today not to let that beautiful shoe box sit in a closet, under a bed, or under a bushel. Let your light so shine before men, that they may see your good works, and glorify your Father which is in heaven. Blow the dust off of that box and pry it open if you have to with everything within you. Realize the potential that resides within that package and know that it is from God. It is one of kind, it is custom made, and it is just for you!

Allow God to regulate the very thing you hold so dear, and allow Him to be your Guide. God spent six days creating all of creation by His word alone, and everything you need was created in those six days.

You are the temple of the Holy Spirit and God endowed you with power even before the foundation of the world. God wants to use you mightily, so stir up the gifts that reside within you and be that willing vessel. Be not afraid of the unknown, for the unknown is not ready for what you have to bring to the table. "Being confident of this very thing, that he which hath begun a good work in you will perform it until the day of Jesus Christ" (Phil. 1:6).

Decreeing and Declaring

The word *declare* means to say or state something out of one's mouth officially or publicly and confidently. By decreeing a thing, we are acknowledging possession of it. We are acknowledging who we are, whose we are, and how we intend to move about with purpose on purpose.

In the beginning when God created man, He gave him power and dominion over the earth to possess it. In doing this, Adam didn't waste any time in taking his rightful position. He immediately began tending to the garden, naming the animals and even his wife. He heard the word of the Lord, received it, and walked in it.

> And God said, Let us make man in our image, after our likeness: and let them have dominion over the fish of the sea, and over the fowl of the air, and over the cattle, and over all the earth, and over every creeping thing that creepeth upon the earth. So God created man in his own image, in the image of God created he him; male and female created he them. And God blessed them, and God said unto them, Be fruitful, and multiply, and replenish the earth, and subdue it: and have dominion over the fish of the sea, and over the fowl of the air, and over every living thing that moveth upon the earth. (Gen. 1:26-28)

As He did with Adam, God is calling us to a place in which we have great authority and power to shift our thinking to be conducive to what we say. The Bible says to call those things that be not as though they were. Although we may not feel like we currently line up with all the positive declarations listed below, we have to speak them nonetheless. God already sees us in this light, and we have to believe that *God's* word is the only truth that matters.

Declarations

- Declare that you are successful.
- Declare the Word of God over your life.
- Declare that you are an overcomer because of the great God who resides within you.
- Declare that God is the One True God.
- Declare that you are the head and not the tail.
- Declare that you have victory over the enemy.
- Declare that the work of your hands is blessed, your family is blessed, and your business is blessed.
- Declare that you will fulfill your destiny come hell or high water, and you will walk out the purpose for which God has placed you on earth.
- Declare that you are more than a conqueror through Jesus Christ.

Declare the Word of God over your destiny and dreams. Allow God to show you what is expedient for this season and time of your life, to ensure you are not moving prematurely on what He has shown you. Remind your spirit daily who God says that you are so that you never fail to believe and walk in it.

God loves you with an everlasting love, and He wants you to prosper and be in health even as your soul prospers. You will experience highs and lows in your life, but trust in the fact that God is constant. He will never change, and He will not change His mind about you. His promises are yea and amen, and He will never leave you nor forsake you. God knows your past, your present, and your future. He is able to redeem that which seems to be lost, and He can do what is seemingly impossible. "Trust in the Lord with all your heart and lean not unto thine own understanding. In all thy ways acknowledge him, and he shall direct thy paths" (Prov. 3:5-6).

Reflect on the scriptures listed below and trust that God is able to do all things. He is always with you, even when you may question whether or not He's there. Be empowered by the Word of God, for it will be the principal thing that will lead you to the path of *understanding, wisdom, fulfillment,* and *success*. Speak it until you believe it and get it deep down in your spirit, for surely you are God's chosen, God's elite, and God's beloved.

Understanding

"For the weapons of our warfare are not carnal, but mighty through God to the pulling down of strong holds" (2 Cor. 10:4).

"Nay, in all these things we are more than conquerors through him that loved us" (Rom. 8:37).

"He giveth power to the faint; and to them that have no might he increaseth strength. Even the youths shall faint and be weary, and the young men shall utterly fall: But they that wait upon the Lord shall renew their strength; they shall mount up with wings as eagles; they shall run, and not be weary; and they shall walk, and not faint" (Isa. 40:29-31).

Wisdom

"And Jesus looking upon them saith, With men it is impossible, but not with God: for with God all things are possible" (Mark 10:27).

"Heaven and earth shall pass away, but my words shall not pass away" (Matt. 24:35).

"I will praise thee; for I am fearfully and wonderfully made: marvellous are thy works; and that my soul knoweth right well" (Ps. 139:14).

Fulfillment

"For I know the thoughts that I think toward you, saith the Lord, thoughts of peace, and not of evil, to give you an expected end" (Jer. 29:11).

"For my God shall supply all my needs according to His riches and glory by Christ Jesus" (Phil. 4:19).

"Come unto me, all ye that labour and are heavy laden, and I will give you rest. Take my yoke upon you, and learn of me; for I am meek and lowly in heart: and ye shall find rest unto your souls" (Matt. 11:28-29).

"And he said unto me, My grace is sufficient for thee: for my strength is made perfect in weakness. Most gladly therefore will I rather glory in my infirmities, that the power of Christ may rest upon me" (2 Cor. 12:9).

Success

"But lay up for yourselves treasures in heaven, where neither moth nor rust doth corrupt, and where thieves do not break through nor steal: For where your treasure is, there will your heart be also" (Matt. 6:20-21).

"So shall my word be that goeth forth out of my mouth: it shall not return unto me void, but it shall accomplish that which I please, and it shall prosper in the thing whereto I sent it" (Isa. 55:11).

God lives in us and because of this, we have a great responsibility to live by faith and not by sight. We should never base our decisions on what is seen alone, but we must also take into account what is not seen. For there is destiny ahead, and only we can walk through its uniquely crafted doors tailored just for us. We must declare life over our purpose and cause our dreams to breathe. If needed, give that purpose CPR as if your life depended on it, because it does. We will forever feel unaccomplished and unfulfilled if we do not walk out the plan God has for us. Only what we do for Christ will last, so breathe! In this moment and in this time in your life, give God your absolute best and let Him do the rest!

"I am crucified with Christ: nevertheless I live; yet not I, but Christ liveth in me: and the life which I now live in the flesh I live by the faith of the Son of God, who loved me, and gave himself for me" (Gal. 2:20).

Who Are You?

At the end of every chapter, there will be a running list based on the scripture references in each chapter of the book about who God says you are. This list can get rather long, so I hope you're ready.
- The Holy People – Isaiah 62:12
- Sought Out – Isaiah 62:12
- A City Not Forsaken – Isaiah 62:12
- More than a Conqueror – Romans 8:37
- Fearfully and Wonderfully Made – Psalm 139:14
- Crucified with Christ – Galatians 2:20

Chapter 2
CONFESSING, REVEALING, AND FACING

I remember the days when my friend and I would mull over the intricate details of our foodfessions. Foodfessions, as I like to call them, are confessions about the deepest, darkest accounts of what one does to get food, eat food, and how it all made him or her feel after the fact. Some may or may not be able to relate to this term; however, people who can know exactly what I mean. These accounts on food have everything to do with a term that I believe is renowned in the world today—*addiction*.

Addiction is such a harsh term when one first hears it and even more of a bitter pill for one to swallow when she has to admit it. Yes, my name is Monique Beck and I have been found guilty of being a food addict. You see, the words can just roll off of my lips now, but it took years for me to come to this realization. I did not fully grasp the fact that the sin of being a glutton was not only killing me physically, it was also destroying my destiny.

As I'll go into greater detail in my next book, *Food Is Good . . . But It's Not Worth Dying For*, food addiction is a very real issue in the world today. People ignore it and believe that it is no big deal because it's *only* food. The truth is, however, that many are dying, getting sick, losing feet, legs, and the like every day due to its repercussions.

Confiding in someone who I knew would not judge me helped me through my process. Hearing myself speak those words out loud was rough, but it helped me to face my reality. It refueled my vigor for life and God's greater plan for my purpose. It gave me the healing power I needed to accept what I had done and what I needed to do to move beyond that point.

Sin has no power over me and sin has no power over you! There is a thin line between sinfulness and righteousness, and it's called a choice. We always have the choice to do right or to do wrong. Sin's wages (no matter what shape, form, or kind) is death according to the Bible. We need to confess our sin, get away from it, and get on with our lives! If we choose not to change, that's fine, but we have to understand that the blood of the other people who were dependent on our choice will be on our hands.

Destiny is not about us solely, but it is about how our destinies affect our children, our children's children and the kingdom of God. We can choose to be selfish and not do anything at all, or we can take the higher road and do something for the greater God who resides in us. Once we do, it will be far easier to confess who God is, who we are in God, and what we are going to do about it.

Confessing

Confession is not only good for the soul, as some people say, but it is also good for the spirit man (the spiritual part of a person). When we think about confession, we often think it means merely referencing things, thoughts, or actions we've done wrong. Confession, however, is also recognizing who God is and who we are in the sight of God. In this chapter, we will look at several ways to confess.

Yes, We Sinned and We Messed up...

Some of us willingly and knowingly ignored the voice of God by not stepping out on what He called us to do. We ignored the burning passion and desire placed inside of us to operate in a specific place in ministry, in business, and even in our families. Yes, some of us did not take on that leadership role, we did not speak up when we should have, and we did not put in the work needed to accomplish our goals. We did not walk through the door that God opened, and we found everything else more important and became busybodies in our own right. We became content with the feeling of under-accomplished. The list goes on and on, but I'm going to stop it here because it's okay. We cannot undo what has already been done, but we *can* do something about what is to be done.

So if you are one of the people who messed up and now are out of sync with where you should be in life, take a pause and apologize. We not only owe ourselves an apology, but we also owe God an apology. We need to go before God and truly seek His forgiveness. God does not live in yesterday, and His promises are yes and amen. He wants us to prosper even as our souls prosper, but we have to be active participants in the prosperity. It is never a good habit to ignore God because He is our Life Source. Ignoring God is like not having blood flowing through your veins. Ultimately, it will end in a natural and spiritual death.

When we take a closer look at the word *sin*, we find that it means an offence or a missing of the mark. Man was born with a sinful nature and is prone to offend God, others, and even himself. Iniquity, however, is continued, unrepented sin. It means perversity, depravity (moral wickedness), and fault. It delves deeper into the inner man and causes him to become less and less sensitive to the things of God. As he becomes comfortable with doing the wrong thing, he becomes contrary, he becomes perverse, and he becomes unfearful of God. He falls away from the living Word of God, and moral wickedness becomes his portion.

When we really take inventory of our lives, we can find all types of things we feel need to be improved; however, there may be some things that we are not aware need to be changed. What we may not see are the tolerances we have developed for "small sins." We may not recognize these acceptances as iniquities, but God does. All sin is sin and is detestable in the sight of the Lord. Whether it be laziness, rebellion, disobedience, molestation, eating those couple of unpaid for cherries at the grocery store, or murder—it is all the same to God. God knows that we all have fallen short of the glory of God, but He doesn't desire that we stay there.

Today is the day and now is the time to rededicate yourself to the Life Source. Release the sin that has so easily beset you! Call it out by name, and cast it down in the mighty name of Jesus! Some sinfulness is more obvious than others, while iniquities are consuming—making their way to the heart of a man. The common thread, however, is that no sin or iniquity can be hidden from God. Repent, get right with God, and get to work! It's not over until God says it's over! Ask God to help you see the small fox that comes to destroy the vine in your life. His time of destroying has expired, and your time is now!

"I acknowledged my sin unto thee, and mine iniquity have I not hid. I said, I will confess my transgressions unto the Lord, and thou forgavest the iniquity of my sin" (Ps. 32:5).

"He that covereth his sins shall not prosper, but whoso confesseth and forsaketh them shall have mercy" (Prov. 28:13).

Confession One to Another

It is sometimes hard for us to admit to ourselves that we have issues, but when we have to admit our faults to someone else. . . . That is a statement that doesn't even need a full response because other people knowing our personal business sometimes makes us cringe. The Bible, however, states that we should practice this type of confession so that we can be healed. What it does not state is that we have to tell our problems to anyone who would listen, but we should rather confess our sins to those who have the ability to pray for and with us.

> "Confess your faults one to another, and pray one for another that ye may be healed. The effectual fervent prayer of the righteous man availeth much" (James 5:16).

During your time with God, ask Him to reveal those people in your life with whom you can share. Ask Him to send you a prayer partner with whom you can pray and confess. It will help both of you and keep you encouraged.

Confession of Who God Is

God is a gigantic God who encompasses the entire universe, and there is no place that He is not. He is a consuming fire, and He is able to consume all of our unrighteousness. Aren't you thankful that God is able to heal, deliver, and make you free? Isn't it wonderful to know that our sins are forgiven and that God's love toward us is without condition? Some of us already know this, but we need to be reminded. Oh, yes, God is all that and then some! In this section, we will go straight to the Scriptures to see what else the Bible says about who God is. I'm sure you'll be pleasantly surprised by what you discover, if you didn't know.

God is . . .
- The Lily of the Valley – Song of Solomon 2:1
- The Bright and Morning Star – Revelation 22:16
- Our Provider – Philippians 4:19
- Our Keeper – Psalm 121
- Love – 1 John 4:8
- Holy – Isaiah 6:3
- A Man of War – Exodus 15:3

- God Almighty – Exodus 6:3
- Great – Psalm 95:3
- Strong and Mighty – Job 36:5
- Our Savior – Isaiah 43:11
- Our Healer – Luke 6:7-11
- Our Redeemer – Isaiah 60:16
- I Am that I Am – Exodus 3:14-15
- Alpha and Omega – Revelation 22:12-13
- A Way-Maker – Isaiah 43:18-21
- Our Heavenly Father – Matthew 6:9-13
- Our Comforter – John 14:26
- A Peace Giver – John 14:27
- A Jealous God – Deuteronomy 5:7-10
- The Word of God – John 1:1-3
- God – Genesis 1:1; 35:11; 46:3; Exodus 3:6; Leviticus 11:44; 11:45; Psalm 81:10; Isaiah 43:3; Jeremiah 1:4-5
- Jesus – Isaiah 9:6; John 1; 10:25-30; John 14:9-11; Acts 4:12; Philippians 2:5-7; Colossians 2:9; 2 Thessalonians 3:5-16

Begin to meditate on these scriptures and read them daily. For God is the King of Kings and the Lord of Lords. He is all-powerful, all-knowing, and all-seeing. Recognize and confess who He is to better understand who you are in Him.

Confession of Who You are in God

The beginning of confessing who you are is knowing who God has called and designed you to be. Of course, you are more than a conqueror, which the Word of God states, but what else resides in you? How are you supposed to impact the world for the advancement of the kingdom of God? What are your gifts and talents that you bring to the table? If you don't know or are unsure, ask God to reveal them to you. It's crucial that you know who you are so that you can be the most effective you that you can be.

One thing I know for sure without knowing you personally is that you are not your past. Your mistakes don't define you, nor can they change God's mind about what and who He says you are. You have been bought with a price, as the Bible says in 1 Corinthians 6:20, so glorify God in your body and spirit. You belong to God and He wants you to live a life of fullness and abundance. Please read through the scriptures below and get better acquainted with yourself.

You are...
- Blessed – Deuteronomy 28, Ephesians 1:3
- A New Creature in Christ – 2 Corinthians 5:17
- Loved – 1 Thessalonians 1:4, Ephesians 2:4-5, Romans 8:37-39
- God's Workmanship – Ephesians 2:8-10
- More than a Conqueror – Romans 8:37-39
- A Son of God – John 1:12
- Stress-free – 1 Peter 5:6-7
- The Temple of the Holy Ghost – 1 Corinthians 6:17-20
- An Heir with Christ – Romans 8:9-17
- An Ambassador of Christ – 2 Corinthians 5:20
- Free – Galatians 5:1
- The Righteousness of God in Him – 2 Corinthians 5:21
- The Body of Christ – 1 Corinthians 12:18-27
- The Light of the World – Matthew 5:14-16
- Covered in Prayer by Jesus – Romans 5:8
- Born of God and Victorious – 2 John 5:1-6

Revealing

When we have the understanding of who God is and who we are in God, we can sit back and reflect on the greater plan that God has in store for His children. We have purpose and we were predestined before the foundation of the world to do great and magnificent things. We no longer have to wonder if God wants to use us, but rather in what capacity. When we seek God, He will reveal to us what our portion is and how we ought to walk into it.

In my quiet time with God, and as I continue throughout my relationship with God, He shows me glimpses of what I should be doing and where I am headed. Although I will never see the full vision/plan, God gives me enough to aspire towards. The Bible says, "Eye hath not seen, nor ear heard, neither have entered into the heart of man, the things which God hath prepared for them that love him" (1 Cor. 2:9).

While writing this book, God showed me myself in so many different capacities in which He wants me to operate. As He poured into me, I began to write down what I saw and heard from Him. I was amazed, to say the least, by what God had shared. As I looked down at the paper, I realized that I could only do those things with the help of God—period. Without God, that list would forever be incomplete and you would not be reading these words today.

When you seek God, ask Him to reveal Himself to you. Communing with God helps one to better recognize His voice and His presence. Spending time in God's Word gives one a better understanding of how she fits into His plan. Prepare yourself before going before the Lord by removing all doubt, distraction, and anything that threatens to pull you away from truth. Empty yourself, so that you may be filled.

Records of Revelations in the Bible

In the book of Hebrews, it is recorded that in times past God spoke to the fathers by the prophets, but in *these* last days He is speaking to us through His Son, Jesus. Jesus is speaking to us directly, and He allows us access to seek Him for ourselves. We no longer have to rely on someone else to do it for us. Through Jesus' death on the cross and the shedding

Confessing, Revealing, and Facing

of His blood, we have life, liberty, and freedom. *Please read Hebrews 9* before continuing on to the next section.

Can you imagine life in the times when people were dependent on the high priest to seek God on their behalf? The tabernacle of God had a special place in it called the Holy of Holies. This was a place where only the high priest could enter once a year to seek atonement for the people's sins. If the priest was not in right standing with God, he would not make it back out alive. This was because the very presence of God resided in that place. *Please read Leviticus 9* for more detailed information on this process.

Now that the veil has been torn through the death of Jesus Christ (glory to God), we can go to God for ourselves. God can forgive us, restore us, and put us back on the right path. He will most definitely reveal Himself to us if we seek Him with our whole heart (see Jer. 29:13).

It is important to note that no one has ever seen the face of God and lived (see Ex. 33:20). Moses spent a lot of time with God while he was obtaining instructions for the people and obtaining the Ten Commandments. When he came back down from Mt. Sinai, his face was glowing and the people were afraid to come near him. God didn't allow Moses to see His face, but He allowed Moses to experience His glory in passing. He actually put a veil over his face to cover it in the midst of the people and he removed it when he spoke with God. Just like Moses, when we have spent time with God, it is noticeable. It can be seen by the way we look, how we carry ourselves, how we speak, and most of all—how we behave. *Please read Exodus 34* for more details on Moses' experience in God's presence.

The following are some other people in the Bible with whom God had intimate relationships:

- **Adam** – God communicated directly with Adam and gave him instructions on how to operate in the garden of Eden. When Adam sinned and fell short of the glory of God after eating the

forbidden fruit, he hid from the presence of God. *Please read Genesis 2-5.*
- **Noah** – Noah was seen as an upright man in the sight of the Lord and God established His covenant with him. God gave Noah instructions to build an ark and Noah followed all that He commanded. Because of his obedience, God spared his family and replenished the earth after the flood. *Please read Genesis 6-9.*
- **Abraham** – Abraham was named by God "the father of many nations." Abraham had a unique relationship with God and he got instructions, direction, and guidance throughout his life due to his interactions with the Lord. *Please read Genesis 11-25 to see his story.*
- **Jesus** – Jesus walked on the earth for thirty-three years and interacted directly with mankind. He was very close with His disciples, and He was right there with them. Jesus taught them how to pray, fast, teach, heal, deliver, and make free. *Please read Matthew, Mark, Luke, and John to see how He lived and what* He did.

Facing

In this chapter, our focus was on confession and revealing. We discovered or were reminded of who God is, who God says we are, and the power of confession in our lives. We saw examples of interactions between God and man and how different each relationship was. Lastly, we were reminded that even when we fall (which we will do or have done), God is there to graciously dust us off, redirect us, and love us with an unconditional love. God wants to use us mightily for His purposes. Let's face it—God has taken away every excuse and He has, therefore, commanded us to live and thrive.

Take time to seek God and ask Him to reveal Himself to you. God can use any person, place, or thing to show Himself mighty and strong in your life. God is a spirit and we have a responsibility to know the

Confessing, Revealing, and Facing

Spirit of God (see 1 John 4:1-6). Examine yourself so that you are certain that there is nothing hindering you from an intimate relationship with God the Father. He desires to spend time with us; however, we need to be sure that we have not placed all the cares of the world before Him. With God being at the top of our list of priorities, we must place those other things in their proper order.

Take about fifteen minutes every day, before the day gets away from you, to think about your priorities for *that* day. If you get into the habit of writing down what you do or would like to do in the course of twenty-four hours, you will have a better visual of how your time is spent. Oftentimes, we think we do not have time to spend with God, we do not have time to spend pursuing our destinies, and we do not have time to do the things of God. My only question is this: What *do* we have time for if we do not have time for the things in which we are promised to have success, fulfillment, and eternal life? Below is an example of how your Daily Agenda can be started.

Daily Agenda

Date: _____   Awake @_____   Asleep @ _____

1. _____
2. _____
3. _____
4. _____
5. _____
6. _____
7. _____
8. _____

Daily Reflections:

_____

_____

Who Are You?

- The Holy People – Isaiah 62:12
- Sought Out – Isaiah 62:12
- A City Not Forsaken – Isaiah 62:12
- More than a Conqueror – Romans 8:37
- Fearfully and Wonderfully Made – Psalm 139:14v
- Crucified with Christ – Galatians 2:20
- Blessed – Ephesians 1:3
- A New Creature in Christ – 2 Corinthians 5:17
- Loved – John 3:16
- God's Workmanship – Ephesians 2:10
- A Son of God – Romans 8:14
- Stress-free – Jeremiah 17:7-8
- The Temple of the Holy Ghost – 1 Corinthians 6:19
- An Heir with Christ – Romans 8:16-17
- An Ambassador of Christ – Ephesians 6:19-20
- Free – Galatians 5:1
- The Righteousness of God in Him – 2 Corinthians 5:21
- The Body of Christ – 1 Corinthians 12:1-27
- The Light of the World – Matthew 5:14-16
- Covered in Prayer by Jesus – Romans 8:26-27
- Born of God – 1 John 4:7
- Victorious – 1 Corinthians 15:57
- Predestined – Romans 8:29-31

Chapter 3
UNDERSTANDING, SEARCHING OUT, AND SEEKING GOD

During my time of confessing, revealing, and facing, as we discussed in the last chapter, God truly allowed me to have a front-row view of how others see me. God showed me the beam that was hanging from my eye like the biggest boulder imaginable. I witnessed the battles, the struggles, the shortcomings, the weaknesses, and the shame. The façade I had placed in front of my phony smile began to get harder and harder to uphold. I was losing it, and I needed to be delivered. Past hurts, hindrances, and self-afflictions ruled my day and death was setting up center stage.

I felt like a shell of my prior self, who had previously been so on fire for Christ. I felt in my heart and spirit that I was moving farther and farther away from the things of God and I needed a refreshing. When I was out of work and didn't have much to do or at work with less to do, I would spend a lot of time reading God's Word. I would pray regularly, fast regularly, and just try to live righteously. What I found, however, was that when I got busy doing other things, I put God to the side. I was missing church, I didn't want to sing on the praise team, and I had gotten very focused on doing my own thing. I was chasing something

I would never obtain on my own—fulfillment. I was trying to do too much by myself, and I forgot that it was only God who lent me the breath I breathed.

Although what I witnessed seemed quite treacherous (and it was), I was lovingly reminded by God that there is no condemnation in Christ Jesus. I understood then that no one, including myself, could ever separate me from the love of God. I felt a sense of peace and conviction in my spirit both at the same time. I knew that God loved me and there was nothing I could do about it.

Today, I can look back on those dark days and simply say, "Thank You, Lord!" I thank God for those feelings that flooded my spirit, letting me know that something was not right. The only way I can explain how I felt is to compare it to a woman having a child. Similar to the contractions she has when her body is preparing to go into labor, my spirit was vexed with a pain. I thank God that He did not leave me in the pit on which my eyes were set and He did not turn me over to a reprobate or morally depraved mind. Only God can change us, and only He can do what may seem impossible to men. When we have a true understanding for what that really means, we find that our issues are nothing that God cannot handle. We need to let go and give it over to Jesus.

> And the disciples were astonished at his words. But Jesus answereth again, and saith unto them, Children, how hard is it for them that trust in riches to enter into the kingdom of God! It is easier for a camel to go through the eye of a needle, than for a rich man to enter into the kingdom of God. And they were astonished out of measure, saying among themselves, Who then can be saved? And Jesus looking upon them saith, With men it is impossible, but not with God: for with God all things are possible. (Mark 10: 24-27)

Understanding

It has been said many times that all roads lead to Rome. It wasn't until after many days of reflection, self-examination, and focusing that I truly got the revelation behind what this statement implied about the Christian walk. What it does not imply is that we can serve any god (lowercase "g") and still go to heaven. What God revealed to me, however, is that we can do nothing apart from God.

The book of Proverbs says that the fear of the Lord is the beginning of wisdom and the knowledge of the holy is understanding. Understanding is one of the keys to taking destiny by force. One must first know who God is, where God needs him, and depend on God to determine how he is to get there. When you understand, you become more aware of the behaviors that are either negatively or positively affecting your growth.

When God gives you a vision, an idea, or a dream, it should be written down. Pray and ask God to lead and guide you in all truth, and He will reveal to you what needs to be accomplished. There will also be times when God will only give you a command without all the detail. He wants to know that you will put your trust and faith in Him alone. Either way, be obedient and do what thus saith the Lord. If there are a number of things God is requiring of you, and you don't have a clue on where to start, ask God for clarity on how to prioritize and be obedient to His response. God is giving us instruction so that His perfect will can be accomplished. It is not about us; it is about advancing the kingdom of God.

> "But as it is written, Eye hath not seen, nor ear heard, neither have entered into the heart of man, the things which God hath prepared for them that love him" (1 Cor. 2:9).

In the book of John, God points out the vine, the branches, and the significance of them staying connected. This Scripture exhorts the believer to remember and understand from whence his/her help comes. We, as believers in Christ, should never forget who the true Power Source is. Just like your cellphone, tablet, or other electronic device needs to be charged to stay alive, we need God to stay alive. Trust me when I tell you: It is not the world, ourselves, or things from which we draw our provision, sustenance, and abilities. Only God can keep our blood flowing and our spirits flourishing, and only He can give us eternal life. There is no other option or road. Jesus is Rome and the only true Road!

> Abide in me, and I in you. As the branch cannot bear fruit of itself, except it abide in the vine; no more can ye, except ye abide in me. I am the vine, ye are the branches: He that abideth in me, and I in him, the same bringeth forth much fruit: for without me ye can do nothing. If a man abide not in me, he is cast forth as a branch, and is withered; and men gather them, and cast them into the fire, and they are burned. If ye abide in me, and my words abide in you, ye shall ask what ye will, and it shall be done unto you. Herein is my Father glorified, that ye bear much fruit; so shall ye be my disciples. (John 15: 4-8)

Searching Out

As discussed in the previous section, there is no life apart from God. It may seem as though one exists, but it simply is not true. God gives each of us a choice to do whatever we want on earth before we leave this place. Whatever we choose, however, will have either a positive or negative impact on our eternal resting place. David said, "If I ascend up into heaven, thou art there: if I make my bed in hell, behold, thou art there" (Psalm 139:8). In this Psalm, David was expressing the very omnipresence and omnipotence of God. God searches and seeks out His sheep. He knows them fully, and they know His voice. Just like God searches us, we have a responsibility to search ourselves. God created each of us for a distinct reason, and it is up to us to discover what that is.

Understanding, Searching Out, and Seeking God

"I the Lord search the heart, I try the reins, even to give every man according to his ways, and according to the fruit of his doings" (Jer. 17:10).

Searching out is a personal affair. It is something that everyone does, whether knowingly or unknowingly. We all, believers and unbelievers alike, have a desire to have clarity and understanding about why we were created. We need to know that what we do matters and that it has value. We sometimes search ourselves, however, we don't always search the scriptures to find our true purpose. We look for signs and indications that we should be in a place, rather than knowing beyond a shadow of a doubt that we were called to a place. Trust me, there is a difference.

Once we get the instructions from God, we need to make certain that God is *always* getting the glory. We don't want to say that we are doing something for God when God is far from it and it doesn't line up with His Word. If God is not in our works, they are in vain. We have to check our motives and be sure we are not doing things to be seen of men. We can never go wrong by laboring in the Lord, and God will be pleased by our works when they are motivated by Him.

"Therefore, my beloved brethren, be ye stedfast, unmoveable, always abounding in the work of the Lord, forasmuch as ye know that your labour is not in vain in the Lord" (1 Cor. 15:58).

When the time comes for each of us to give an individual account of our lives to God, there will be no withholding. He will know all because He has seen all. We will definitely be held accountable for walking out our purpose or not walking out our purpose—so we may as well do it right! Examine yourself to be sure you are in the faith. You only have one lifetime, no matter how short or long it is, to live out your destiny. Spend some time taking a spiritual inventory and search yourself. If you find that you have fallen off track, get back on track and ask God to forgive you. While you still have breath, you still have an opportunity to give everything you have for Christ.

> "Examine yourselves, whether ye be in the faith; prove your own selves. Know ye not your own selves, how that Jesus Christ is in you, except ye be reprobates?" (2 Cor. 13:5).

Seeking God

As believers in Christ, it is our duty to spend time getting to know God, our heavenly Father. In our quest of seeking out God, we can expect to be met, restored, informed, and refreshed. On our walk into our destinies, we cannot expect to be on the trail alone. We have to learn of the One who promised to carry us the whole way through. In seeking Christ and in communing with Him, we gain a better understanding of who He is, who we are in Him, and how we ought to live our lives on earth. When we truly fellowship with God, our lives are visibly changed, and our faith is taken to higher heights.

> "But if from thence thou shalt seek the Lord thy God, thou shalt find him, if thou seek him with all thy heart and with all thy soul" (Deut. 4:29).

Through the Word of God

One proven way to find God is in His Word, as He is the Word (see John 1:1). The Bible is filled with God's attributes, character traits, relationships with His creation, instructions in righteousness, and a myriad of prophecies. In the Word of God, we find correction, rebuke, promises, and the story of creation and redemption. Jesus teaches us how to pray and how not to pray; how to love; how to have a good marriage; how to raise children and even how to live for Him. Although it would be wonderful if God would download all of this into us in one sitting, it is not so. We must set time aside daily to get into His presence.

There is no perfect way of reading God's Word. Some people say that one should start with the four Gospels (Matthew, Mark, Luke, and John). Others say that one should start at the beginning in Genesis. I say that in whatever you do, do it for the glory of God. There will be times when you are studying God's Word that you'll be searching more for understanding rather than an answer. At other times, you may be seeking to find a scripture or passage that will help with a particular situation with which you are faced. Whatever the reason, read the Word and stick with it. For God's Word is a lamp unto our feet and a light unto our paths (see Ps. 119:105).

Through Prayer (Communication with God)

Prayer, simply stated, is communication with God. It is a conversation between the Creator and His creation. It is a time for God's people to have an intimate or unified conversation with God the Father. Because the veil has been rent (torn), we have direct access to talk to God one-on-one with nothing holding us back but ourselves. When Jesus died on the cross, we received permission to enter the holiest place with boldness (see Heb. 10:16-23). We can communicate with Jesus through prayers of praise, worship, confession, thanksgiving, intercession, and supplication (Hunt and King, 2001).

In the book of 1 Thessalonians, the Bible says that we ought to pray without ceasing and in everything we should give thanks. This may seem to be an impossible task for some, but it isn't. If we really sat down and took an inventory of our interactions throughout the day, we would see the opportunities we had to turn complaints to confessions and worries to worship. We would see that in the time we spent panicking about what we were going to do about a situation, we could have praised God for being able to fix every situation. Spending time with God in prayer is life-changing and it is evident when it is absent in the life of a believer. Omitting prayer from our lives is like omitting air from our lungs. We must spend less time doubting God and more time depending on God.

God will fulfill every promise He gave to us. He wants to provide for every need we have and He wants to be our first option, not our last resort. He wants us to come to Him just like a son would to his father.

> "God is not a man, that he should lie; neither the son of man, that he should repent: hath he said, and shall he not do it? or hath he spoken, and shall he not make it good" (Num. 23:19).

Scriptures on Promises through Prayer

- Deuteronomy 4:7 – God is available
- Matthew 7:7-12 – Ask and it shall be given
- Mark 11:24-26 – Believe it and receive it by faith
- Luke 11:9-13 – A promise to find what is sought
- John 14:10-14 – Answered prayer in Jesus' name
- Philippians: 4:6-7 – Don't worry—pray!
- 1 John 5:14-15 – Desired petitions obtained

Through Fasting

The book of Ecclesiastes states that to every thing there is a season, and a time to every purpose under the heaven. Inclusive of "every thing" and "every purpose" (Eccl. 3:1), fasting has its place. According to Dictionary.com, fasting is defined as abstaining from all food or certain kinds of food. Although this definition directly relates to food, some people choose to abstain from things like television, games, sweets, certain types of music, or a myriad of other things. In addition, there are many purposes for fasting in the life of a believer in Christ and things that are obtained from this sacrifice. The essential purpose, however, is to gain a closer relationship with God.

Fasting sometimes seems like an impossible feat, but Jesus showed us through His example that it can be done. In the Bible, people fasted to mourn; to humble themselves before the Lord; to obtain strength; to repent; to worship God; and to discipline their bodies. Fasting breaks

Understanding, Searching Out, and Seeking God

down the body in a sense, but it helps the believer to become more sensitive to the Holy Spirit. It allows for a separation from the cares of the world in order to get clear direction from God.

As the definition on fasting omitted accurately, there is not a specified amount of time in which it should be completed. This is a decision that should be led by God and done for the glory of God. Some people may fast for twelve hours, while others may abstain from food for a period of twelve days. Whatever length of time given by God, it will be a stint that the person can accomplish. Praying, reading the Word, and depending on God will be critical in receiving strength to finish.

> Moreover when ye fast, be not, as the hypocrites, of a sad countenance: for they disfigure their faces, that they may appear unto men to fast. Verily I say unto you, They have their reward. But thou, when thou fastest, anoint thine head, and wash thy face; that thou appear not unto men to fast, but unto thy Father which is in secret: and thy Father, which seeth in secret, shall reward thee openly. (Matt. 6:16-18)

Let's face it—fasting will not be an easy undertaking. The flesh (the body) does not like to be told "no" to anything it has become accustomed to having or seemingly needs. Food is a necessity in life, but it won't kill a person to turn down a plate or two temporarily. There are some people who may not be able to fast without food due to medical reasons and God understands that. Just know that in whatever type of fast is undertaken, rely on God for all you need and consult with your doctor to determine if any other supplements/vitamins are needed while you are on your journey of seeking God.

One of the first fasts I did was with my church's co-pastor. She and I fasted for seven full days with no food. We drank juice when it got hard, but other than that, no food. Was it challenging? Absolutely, but we made it through! It seemed impossible at the time as the days progressed, but I was reminded that I could do all things through Christ who strengthened me.

Trust me—practice does not make perfect even if one considers himself a "veteran" at fasting. When one truly fasts for God, it is a sacrifice and the enemy will present himself in one way or another. The flesh, however, does get a better understanding of Who's in charge. While you are on your journey of getting clarity from God, understanding your purpose, checking off your to-do lists, and making your calling and election sure—be encouraged. Temptation will come and the very thing you are trying to avoid will be on the forefront. God, however, will not allow you be tempted above what you are able. God is faithful and He will make a way for you to escape.

> There hath no temptation taken you but such as is common to man: but God is faithful, who will not suffer you to be tempted above that ye are able; but will with the temptation also make a way to escape, that ye may be able to bear it. (1 Cor. 10:13)

Scriptures on Fasting
- 1 Samuel 7:6; Joel 2:12-13 – Repentance
- Ezra 8:21-23 – Strength in prayer
- Esther 4:3 – Mourning
- Psalm 35:13; James 4:10 – Humbling oneself
- Matthew 4:1-11 – Jesus' example of fasting
- Matthew 17:20-22 – Deliverance
- Luke 2:37 – Worship
- Acts 14:23 – Guidance from the Holy Spirit
- Romans 12:1-2 – A living sacrifice to God
- 1 Corinthians 6:19-20, 9:27 – Discipline

Who Are You?

- The Holy People – Isaiah 62:12
- Sought Out – Isaiah 62:12
- A City Not Forsaken – Isaiah 62:12
- More than a Conqueror – Romans 8:37
- Fearfully and Wonderfully Made – Psalm 139:14
- Crucified with Christ – Galatians 2:20
- Blessed – Ephesians 1:3
- A New Creature in Christ – 2 Corinthians 5:17
- Loved – John 3:16
- God's Workmanship – Ephesians 2:10
- A Son of God – Romans 8:14
- Stress-free – Jeremiah 17:7-8
- The Temple of the Holy Ghost – 1 Corinthians 6:19
- An Heir with Christ – Romans 8:16-17
- An Ambassador of Christ – Ephesians 6:19-20
- Free – Galatians 5:1
- The Righteousness of God in Him – 2 Corinthians 5:21
- The Body of Christ – 1 Corinthians 12:1-27
- The Light of the World – Matthew 5:14-16
- Covered in Prayer by Jesus – Romans 8:26-27
- Born of God – 1 John 4:7
- Victorious – 1 Corinthians 15:57
- Predestined – Romans 8:29-31
- The Branches – John 15:5

Chapter 4
UNDERSTANDING ACCEPTANCE

As a child, I had a speech impediment and stuttered severely. It was quite an embarrassing time for me and would often make me feel paralyzed when I tried to speak. I loved to sing (and still do) as well and never stuttered when I did that, so stuttering while speaking may forever be a mystery to me. In any case, the words would form in my head and I would be so excited to utter them. This, sadly, would often produce a repetition of the same word over and over again. Some of the kids would tease me, and at the time it was challenging to overcome. My mother continuously gave me tips on how to slow down, think about what I wanted to say, and then speak. I also began seeing a speech therapist.

As I got older and attended my first year of college, I continued to stutter. I was very shy and would not speak at times when I felt the stuttering was going to manifest. I will never forget during that first year, I wanted to be on the dean's list. I strived to get a 4.0. I had all As except for one class—my public speaking class where I got a B. I was mortified on that first day of class when we were presented with an impromptu speech. For those who may not know what that is, an impromptu speech is a speech that is done without preparation. It is completely spontaneous. I told my teacher I simply could not do it because of the fear of judgment. After I received that big fat zero, I knew it was something I had to overcome. The remainder of the speeches I did in that class were done while I was shaking, knees knocking, and stuttering happening. I had to do what I had to do.

It's amazing how little I stutter today, but it is not totally gone. I think of it as a reminder of how much I need God and am dependent on Him. He continuously helps me to see that it's not by might, nor by power but by His Spirit. I never want to get so high-minded and confident in my own abilities that I forget that it was God who did it.

I have accepted my weakness and am thankful that God allows me to express myself freely in diverse situations with His help. God called me to teach the Word of God, and before I could do that I had to overcome my fear of rejection. Even today when I stutter, it often takes people off guard. Some people try to ignore it, while others make faces. Either way, I don't let it stop me from saying what needs to be said. God helped me to realize that my obedience was greater than my sacrifice, and that my stuttering would not be an excuse for me not to preach the gospel and share the good news.

Acceptance

There are times in our lives when acceptance by others reigns supreme. In our teen years and even as adults, we sometimes wrestle with the way people think about us and are often affected by how people quantify our value. These two things have the potential to cause one to become stagnate, to forget about his purpose in life, to have low self-esteem, and to be filled with self-doubt. Jesus has come, however, so that we may have life and that more abundantly. He will accept us and love us no matter what we do, look like, say, or think. Because He's God, He changes not. He will always love His people with an everlasting, inescapable love. In this, we must not let other people's opinions dictate what we can and cannot do. If God gave you a yes, that settles it.

> Who shall separate us from the love of Christ? shall tribulation, or distress, or persecution, or famine, or nakedness, or peril, or sword? As it is written, For thy sake we are killed all the day long; we are accounted as sheep for the slaughter. Nay, in all these things we are more than conquerors through him that loved us. (Rom. 8:35-37)

Acceptance by Others

Some people say there is no greater bond than the one between a husband and his wife, for they have become one flesh, forsaken all others, and decided that they would stay together for better or for worse. They spend time getting to know each other, and the years begin to add up day by day. They feel inseparable and truly believe in their hearts that there is nothing that anyone can tell them about their spouse that they do not already know. The truth is, however, that even in marriage there is always something to be learned or discovered. It is not possible for one person to know everything about another, even if they worked on it twenty-four hours a day.

Only God knows all things concerning you and not even you know you like He knows you. Sounds funny when you think about it, but it's true. The computer was made by man and has no understanding in and of itself. It is the one who created it who knows its inner workings. Accept what God says about you, and put your faith and trust in what He has promised you. Only His opinion really matters.

One of the key phrases coined for this time period is "Keep it real!" or "Keep it 100". If this was being practiced on a daily basis, would it be necessary for anyone to say it? Could people actually handle 100 percent of the real us? Often in conversations and interactions with others, we have a tendency to withhold things, knowingly or unknowingly. We sometimes do this because we don't want to put the other person in a position to judge us or because we are afraid of how he/she will react to what we have done. We only reveal enough to make the story believable but not condemning. Why do we do this? Why do we still have fear about what our truth can mean for us? Why do we constantly look at another person's facial expressions when we speak to see if we can trust them with the rest of the story? Are we not comfortable with who we are? Have we accepted who God says we are?

In essence, it is only God's thoughts toward us that carry eternal weight. Yes, we may go through some things because of the seeds we have sown on earth, but God has a sure enough Word and purpose for us! No matter what other people's testimonies are concerning us. God will have the final say concerning *all* these things!

Acceptance by God

Take a few minutes to think about all the things you know about yourself and what others know about you. Take another minute to think about the things that others *don't* know about you. Do you have the visual? Did you know that the very hairs on your head are numbered and that God knows that number? Did you know that only God knows your heart? Not even you can say that you truly know your heart nor can you trust it. What we think we know about ourselves—we don't know. What others think they know about us—they don't know. Only God knows.

The book of Jeremiah says, "The heart is deceitful above all things, and desperately wicked: who can know it?" (Jer. 17:5). It is because of this that we must rely fully on God for understanding, acceptance, and wisdom. If it is possible for our hearts to lead us to denial, corruption, and wickedness, how much more should we not depend on it to lead us to good things? I point this out to say, we cannot follow our hearts when it comes to destiny or anything in life. We must follow Christ who *is* destiny and life. For God has thoughts of good and not of evil concerning us, and He is the Good Shepherd. He is trustworthy and we can put our lives in His hands. He accepts us, so we should therefore accept ourselves.

Only God knows the complete inner workings of man. Doctors have searched and will continue to search for years and years to come, and they will never have a full understanding of how God's creation works. They may discover things along the way, but only the Creator truly knows His creation and reveals what He sees fit. So with this in mind, we must remember that we cannot fault others for not being God. We cannot hold them accountable for not knowing us as people, and we should not be completely surprised when something disappointing takes place. People only know what they see and what God allows to be revealed. Man looks at the outward appearance, but only God looks at the actual heart.

Self-Acceptance

What would you do if you knew everything there is to know about yourself and exactly what would happen in your life? I would have to imagine this would put you in a great position of power and could be very damaging to you. It is quite possible that you would chose to be lazy in some areas and advance in others because you would already know the outcome. It is likely that you would decide that God is not necessary in your life until you "actually" need Him. God will reveal your purpose to you, and when He does, accept it and move toward it. You may not get every detail and will have to depend on Him for guidance, but God will not allow you to be in ignorance of your calling.

God promised that He would never leave us nor forsake us. He is absolutely 100 percent sure of who we are in Him, and we must accept that He is 100 percent right. God doesn't make mistakes, and He knows exactly what He planned when He distributed our spiritual gifts. There is no one greater who can confirm who we are and why we exist than God Himself. We were created in His image and likeness to accomplish His perfect will. *Please read 1 Corinthians 12.*

Today, you may not see what God sees in you, but trust Him—it's in there! You have to come into agreement with who God says you are. If not, you are walking in doubt and unbelief. We have to believe and have faith or it will be impossible to please God (see Heb. 11:16). Once we accept it, we must seek to understand our place in this earthly walk.

As we touched on in the beginning of this chapter, we sometimes search for acceptance from people. In the book of Luke, Jesus talks about a prophet not being accepted in his hometown. This lets you know that people will reject you at some time or another. Even Jesus was rejected by the same people who saw Him perform miracles, signs, and wonders, and He is the Son of God! Rejection, then, is to be expected. Our job, however, is not to focus on the rejection, but rather the acceptance by our Lord and Savior Jesus Christ. *Please read Luke 4:14-24.*

A Prayer for Acceptance of God's Call

Dear Heavenly Father,

Help us to continually accept the call and purpose that You have revealed to us by faith. Cause us to be living sacrifices unto You that are both holy and acceptable. Cause us to line up with the mandate You have placed on our lives so that You may be glorified and magnified in our works. For truly, only what we do for Christ will last and we want to please You in every way.

God, teach us how to number our days so that we are not found making excuses, wasting time, and walking in the opposite direction of greatness. For You are the King of Kings and the Lord of Lords. There is none like You in heaven and in earth. We were created in Your image and likeness and were placed on this earth to praise and worship Your name. Open up our eyes so that we may see the course that You have placed before us.

Lord, give us the understanding that the secret things belong only to You. Let Your strength be made perfect in our weakness as we remember from whence our help comes. Cause our faith to go from glory to glory, as we stay connected to You in all things. Help us to fight the good fight of faith and remember that You are always there for us during the good and the bad times. For You are God alone, and Your name will forever reign. Heaven and earth shall pass away, but Your Word will always remain. In Jesus' name, Amen.

Who Are You?

- The Holy People – Isaiah 62:12
- Sought Out – Isaiah 62:12
- A City Not Forsaken – Isaiah 62:12
- More than a Conqueror – Romans 8:37
- Fearfully and Wonderfully Made – Psalm 139:14
- Crucified with Christ – Galatians 2:20
- Blessed – Ephesians 1:3
- A New Creature in Christ – 2 Corinthians 5:17
- Loved – John 3:16
- God's Workmanship – Ephesians 2:10
- A Son of God – Romans 8:14
- Stress-free – Jeremiah 17:7-8
- The Temple of the Holy Ghost – 1 Corinthians 6:19
- An Heir with Christ – Romans 8:16-17
- An Ambassador of Christ – Ephesians 6:19-20
- Free – Galatians 5:1
- The Righteousness of God in Him– 2 Corinthians 5:21
- The Body of Christ – 1 Corinthians 12:1-27
- The Light of the World – Matthew 5:14-16
- Covered in Prayer by Jesus – Romans 8:26-27
- Born of God – 1 John 4:7
- Victorious – 1 Corinthians 15:57

- Predestined – Romans 8:29-31
- The Branches – John 15:5
- Accepted by God – Romans 8:34-37
- Called – Romans 8:28
- Created in the Image and Likeness of God – Genesis 1:26-27

Chapter 5
FORGIVENESS

Have you ever heard the saying, "Never go to bed angry, stay awake and plot your revenge" or "Revenge is best served cold"? Well, there is another saying that I just want to bring to your attention before we begin the section on forgiveness: "Before you begin on the journey of revenge, dig two graves"!

Forgiveness or unforgiveness is one of the defining characteristics that will mark a follower in Christ from those who do not follow Christ. This is not to say that only Christians forgive—Christians must forgive! The first thing Jesus said on the cross, as recorded in Luke 23 was, "Father, forgive them, for they know not what they do". Even to the point of death and giving up the ghost, Jesus had a forgiving spirit. He needed us to know how important it is not to plot revenge and to put our trust in God. The last words He uttered in the same chapter of Luke were, "Father, into thy hands, I commend my spirit"!

Now I know without a doubt that no one reading this book has laid down his/her life for others (who didn't deserve it) and has forgiven them while they were doing it. I know that none of us can say that we understand how Christ, who did no wrong and committed no sin, died a sinner's death for the salvation of others. I know that we can only imagine how challenging it must have been for the man Christ Jesus giving of Himself to accomplish the will of God on earth. Yet, when someone steps on our shoe or takes credit for our ideas, we decide to hold a grudge until "hell freezes over" (which is never going to happen).

I will never forget the time when a supervisor and I argued about something that had nothing to do with anything. It was quite petty, and I believe that we both were trying to get the upper hand. Now here I am, the subordinate, and I'm raising my voice and talking out of turn to someone in authority. At the time, I did not feel that she deserved the title because she was not doing what *I* felt she should be doing as a leader. Being one who is saved, I felt very convicted about the whole thing and had to repent. I was definitely having feelings of animosity toward her and her approach, but I realized that I would forever ruin my witness as a follower of Christ if I did not make it right. I had to go back and apologize and ask her to forgive me for anything I said that was out of order. I may never know if I was able to repair the damage done to our working relationship; however, I felt free from the guilt of having mishandled her as a person in God's creation.

Forgiveness

You are probably wondering why forgiveness comes after a chapter on acceptance, but un-forgiveness is like one holding herself hostage in a prison cell and keeping the keys in her own pocket. Unforgiveness keeps us from living the full life that God intended, as it prevents us from moving forward in relationships, in business, and in ministry. Not only is destiny on the line due to it, but our very relationship with God is deeply affected. We must be free and stay free so that we can effectively impact the areas in which we should be operating. Whether you have never gone to church or been working in ministry for twenty years, we all have the same requirement and forgiveness is a must.

Forgiveness

"For if ye forgive men their trespasses, your heavenly Father will also forgive you: but if ye forgive not men their trespasses, neither will your Father forgive your trespasses" (Matt. 6:14-15).

After reading this verse, we can see the importance of staying free (in a forgivable state). I don't know anyone who would knowingly want to be in a position in which God refuses to forgive them for their sins. If you really take a moment and think about all the wrongs you did just in the course of today and the implications those things have for your eternal resting place—what do you think the conclusion will be?

Imagine that you are harboring unforgiveness in your heart due to some tragic event that happened when you were little. You felt as though you moved on because you got into church and truly became a believer in Jesus Christ. Day by day, you worked to do your absolute best to keep God's commandments, read your Bible, and treat all people with love and respect. One day you mess up so badly that you feel the need to fast and pray to get God's attention. During your time with God, you cry out to Him and ask for forgiveness. After three hours of begging and pleading, you hear God's simple yet definite response—silence. You suddenly begin to feel as though you've wasted your time and immediately the idea enters your mind that God wasn't real in the first place. You begin to lose all confidence in prayer, and you decide that you are just going to do your *own* thing because God doesn't answer prayer.

This may serve as an example for some, but for others it is the reality in which they live. I am here to tell you that it doesn't and will never work. Unforgiveness doesn't hurt the one who committed the offence against you—it hurts you. It is like spiritual suicide that leads to eternal damnation. It is God's job to have vengeance on our enemies, not ours. For certainly the Bible says that what one sows he will also reap, but our job is to love and forgive regardless of wrongdoings. Forgiveness doesn't make us weak as people—it makes us wise and strengthens our relationship with God. It gives us the ability to move forward with purpose. We cannot do anything effectively for God or ourselves when we are holding on to past hurts. We have to get that right first and then we can offer our gift to God.

> "Therefore if thou bring thy gift to the altar, and there rememberest that thy brother hath ought against thee; leave there thy gift before the altar, and go thy way; first be reconciled to thy brother, and then come and offer thy gift" (Matt. 5:23-24).

So what do we do when the same thing that someone did to us in the past happens again? We forgive again! There is no end to forgiveness. In addition to forgiving others in life, we will also need to forgive ourselves for what we have done to ourselves. We will have to seek God for forgiveness and we will have to be forgiven. When Peter asked Jesus how many times should he forgive men their offences, Jesus said seventy times seven. This may seem hard to do, but it is definitely possible. If it weren't so, God would not have told us to do it. Love covers a multitude of sins, and it is far easier to love than to hate. Hate takes work and is cumbersome, but love is liberating and freeing. We must put the past in its place and stretch forward to the greater in our tomorrow.

> "Brethren, I count not myself to have apprehended: but this one thing I do, forgetting those things which are behind, and reaching forth unto those things which are before, I press toward the mark for the prize of the high calling of God in Christ Jesus" (Phil. 3:13-14).

Unforgiveness is like living in the past where nothing can be changed, edited, or fixed. It is like listening to a scratched CD that always skips at the same part of the song. It is old and unproductive. It is a time waster and time consumer. It reaches into the soul of a woman in an attempt to snatch out her potential, her purpose, and her power. It festers, sets up shop, and tries to make its permanent habitat in a place where the Holy Spirit should reside. It is relentless in its pursuit of life, but it is not unstoppable. It is within our power to stop the bleeding and forgive. If we will not allow others to hold us up, certainly we cannot be our own delay. Enough is enough! It is up to us whether or not we want to be free indeed.

How do I Forgive?

Well, it is really simple—just say "I forgive (person's name), for doing (what they did). There will be a weight that is lifted, although it may take several declarations for it to become a reality in your life. Forgiveness is truly something that needs to be practiced on a daily basis. You must speak it, mean it, and do it. It is possible that old feelings may rise up when you are reminded about what happened, but it is all about what you do with those feelings.

The Bible says that we can be angry, but that anger should not cause us to sin. If you are still angry about what happened to you and it is causing you to sin, you haven't truly forgiven. You have to put it in God's hands, and move on with your life.

God is such a good and loving God. When we reflect on who He is and what He desires for us, it helps us to realize how important and precious the time we have on earth is. We do not want to die in unforgiveness and miss out on eternal life with Christ because we could not leave our past in the past. Christ died on the cross one time for our sins, and He is not doing it a second time. He expects us to do what we have to do in this temporary short life that we have on earth so that we can reign with Him in eternity forever and ever.

> "I, even I, am he that blotteth out thy transgressions for mine own sake, and will not remember thy sins. Put me in remembrance: let us plead together: declare thou, that thou mayest be justified" (Isa. 43:25-26).

Sweet, sweet forgiveness . . . It is a requirement and I pray that you have the opportunity to commune and get acquainted with it. Forgive yourself, forgive others, and commit to a life of forgiveness. Understand that you cannot move forward and stay in the same place at the same time. You have to change your course and look from the place that you are. For God desires to give you more.

Where much is given, much is required. You can do this and God can help! Let the burden be lifted in your life because there is a God. He *is* real, He *does* answer prayer, and He *is* a rewarder of them that diligently seek Him.

> Who is a God like unto thee, that pardoneth iniquity, and passeth by the transgression of the remnant of his heritage? he retaineth not his anger for ever, because he delighteth in mercy. He will turn again, he will have compassion upon us; he will subdue our iniquities; and thou wilt cast all their sins into the depths of the sea (Mic. 7:18-19).

Who Are You?

- The Holy People – Isaiah 62:12
- Sought Out – Isaiah 62:12
- A City Not Forsaken – Isaiah 62:12
- More than a Conqueror – Romans 8:37
- Fearfully and Wonderfully Made – Psalm 139:14
- Crucified with Christ – Galatians 2:20
- Blessed – Ephesians 1:3
- A New Creature in Christ – 2 Corinthians 5:17
- Loved – John 3:16
- God's Workmanship – Ephesians 2:10
- A Son of God – Romans 8:14
- Stress-free – Jeremiah 17:7-8
- The Temple of the Holy Ghost – 1 Corinthians 6:19
- An Heir with Christ – Romans 8:16-17

Forgiveness

- An Ambassador of Christ – Ephesians 6:19-20
- Free – Galatians 5:1
- The Righteousness of God in Him – 2 Corinthians 5:21
- The Body of Christ – 1 Corinthians 12:1-27
- The Light of the World – Matthew 5:14-16
- Covered in Prayer by Jesus – Romans 8:26-27
- Born of God – 1 John 4:7
- Victorious – 1 Corinthians 15:57
- Predestined – Romans 8:29-31
- The Branches – John 15:5
- Accepted by God – Romans 8:34-37
- Called – Romans 8:28
- Created in the Image and Likeness of God – Genesis 1:26-27
- Forgiven – Ephesians 4:32

Chapter 6
RESTORATION AND REVITALIZATION

What I discovered after *years* of going around and around about what I couldn't do was that I *could* do *all* things through Christ who gave me the strength. I can say this happened because I'm a slow learner (which is true in some regards), but I don't believe that would be the total truth. In life, we all go through things for a reason and I believe part of that reason is to help someone else who may be dealing with something similar. We also go through things so that God can be glorified and His name made great in the earth!

In my case, I had lost my confidence and had become very unsure of myself. People would always call me smart, but I didn't feel very smart about not knowing what to do with my own life. I did not know what I was good at, and everyone else seemed to have it figured out. The problem wasn't that someone was holding me back, but it was that I did not fully believe God could do it. God restored my confidence and my faith in believing that He had me covered. He knew that I would feel the way I did, and He was right there to help me through it.

So you may ask yourself why God would ever do this and why you have to even get to a point where revitalization is needed. The answer I would offer is this: Why not you? We don't choose Christ—He chooses us. Because we no longer live in the garden of Eden, as noted in the book of Genesis, we are faced with many trials, tribulations, and sufferings. The *man* Christ Jesus walked the earth for thirty-three years, and He faced the same things we do.

Whether we ever decide to follow Christ or not, we will still go through the issues of life. It is up to us to decide if we will serve Him, believe Him, trust Him, live for Him, and reap the benefits of being connected to Him. God is just and will not make us go after the reward that is waiting for us when we decide to follow Him. That choice is ours.

In the end, if we are obedient to His voice, we and others are blessed beyond measure. Do I have bad days and fall short? Yes, I do! Am I going to wallow in my guilt, doubt, and disobedience? No, I will not! God is capable and able to do anything we ask in His name according to His will. My prayer is that you will never be the same.

Restoration

Freedom! Freedom! Freedom! Yessss!! Walk in the light on the path that God has set before you. God is renewing, restoring, and reviving all the things that the enemy tried to steal. Spiritual health, right relationships, joy, abundance, peace, a sound mind, and the list goes on and on. Believe that He can do it! Whatever held you back before is now null, void, and demolished. You are free to be your best you! For you have seen but a glimpse of the potential that lies within you, and Jesus Himself said that you would do greater works than He did on the earth!

Self-captivity is a thing of the past, as God Himself has made you free! Who can limit you now that God has made you limitless and, if God said it, that settles it! You may not have known before, but you know now that you are God's beloved. You are the apple of His eye, and He wants you to enjoy the place He has gone and prepared for you.

Restoration and Revitalization

Isn't it amazing to know how awesome God is? The reason it seems that we can be down one day and up the next is because God is forever and always in the restoring business! He is the redeemer of the lives of men and a restorer of their very souls. May we never forget His faithfulness and always reverence His name.

> Bless the Lord, O my soul: and all that is within me, bless his holy name. Bless the Lord, O my soul, and forget not all his benefits: who forgiveth all thine iniquities; who healeth all thy diseases; who redeemeth thy life from destruction; who crowneth thee with lovingkindness and tender mercies; who satisfieth thy mouth with good things; so that thy youth is renewed like the eagle's. The Lord executeth righteousness and judgment for all that are oppressed. (Ps. 103:1-6)

In the last chapter, we focused on unloading all that extra baggage and making a decision to walk in peace. We talked about hearkening to the voice of the Lord our God and declaring that all is well with our souls! Don't dwell on the negative things that have taken place in your life, but relish in the good that God has done. Let your life bring glory to the name of the Lord. Walk and don't faint! Run and don't grow weary! For surely your heavenly Father will be there for you and will reward you in due time.

> For he that soweth to his flesh shall of the flesh reap corruption; but he that soweth to the Spirit shall of the Spirit reap life everlasting. And let us not be weary in well doing: for in due season we shall reap, if we faint not. As we have therefore opportunity, let us do good unto all men, especially unto them who are of the household of faith. (Gal. 6:8-10)

Scriptures on Restoration
- Your Soul – Psalm 23:3
- A Renewed Spirit and Clean Heart – Psalm 51:7, 9
- Joy – Psalm 51:12
- Life – Isaiah 38:16-19
- What the Enemy Stole – Joel 2:25-26
- Reconciled to God – 2 Corinthians 5:17-21
- Of All Things – Acts 3:20-21

Revitalization

Is there anything in you that you know is there and may be lying dormant? Is there a spiritual gift, a talent, a desire or passion toward the things of God that hasn't been operating in a while? Have you stopped seeing yourself on a higher level, in a different dimension or at a different place then where you currently are? As you walk along the path of joy, health and a renewed mind and spirit, pray that God will stir up the gifts that He has placed inside of you. This is the acceptable year of the Lord, and He wants you to have victory in it!

Over the years, I struggled with un-forgiveness, addiction and shame. These things weighed heavily on me, as I began to fall further and further into sin. I would be up and on fire for God one day, and a few weeks later dusted and disgusted. I'm not sure if you can relate to this story, but this was my reality for a long time. After so many years of being a "yo-yo Christian" (on again, off again), it dawned on me that I was not getting any younger. I had to do something with what God gave me and I knew that only *I* could do it.

The effects of sin, poor decisions and wrong relationships can take a toll on you emotionally. They can make you feel unworthy, unwanted, unloved and ashamed. The good news, however, is that regardless of how you feel – God still wants to use you. Hallelujah! We cannot dwell on what was and must focus on what is. Taking destiny by force doesn't encompass crying over spilled milk. It recognizes what needs to be done and does something about it. If we just sat around all day and talked about what we were going to do or *about* to do, we would never get anything done.

The book of Romans records that the gifts and callings of God are without repentance. This means that regardless of what we do in life, we cannot escape our God-given purpose. Don't ever stop dreaming and remembering what God showed you. If He showed you something grand, remember that this is only a small part of what He has in store. God sees the person that you are and so does the devil. It is the devil's job to disrupt you and distract you from your destiny by any means necessary. Even he knows the Word of God and believes in the power that resides in you. If he is trying to destroy your purpose, it is only because he knows that you have one.

Tell yourself that you are who God says you are and be that. Take comfort in knowing that He wants to use you for His glory, even if you don't feel that you can be or should be used. Because He is God, He has all power and can do all things.

> "Wherefore I put thee in remembrance that thou stir up the gift of God, which is in thee by the putting on of my hands. For God hath not given us the spirit of fear; but of power, and of love, and of a sound mind. Be not thou therefore ashamed of the testimony of our Lord" (2 Tim. 1:6-8).

Scriptures on Revitalization
- Strength – 1 Kings 19:7-8
- Healing of our Land – 2 Chronicles 7:14
- Spiritual Life – Psalm 116:1-9
- Together with Christ - Ephesians 2:1-5
- Salvation – Titus 3:5-7

A Prayer for Revival

Dear Lord,

I thank You for all that You have done for Your people and for helping us to see that You are the great I Am that I Am. You make our paths straight and are all that we need to live. I thank You for placing Your Holy Spirit inside of us to lead us in all truth.

God, I pray that You will send a revival to Your people so they are able to see what You see in them. Help them to believe that You have called them to a great and mighty work that must be completed in order for them to return to You. Stir up the gifts that You have placed in them so they may effectively play their part in the body of Christ and the kingdom of God. Help them to see that You love them unconditionally and yet have work for them to do. Despite what they have done in their past, You have the power to throw their sins in the sea of forgetfulness.

God, restore all the enemy tried to steal from them. Help them to live, thrive, and press towards the higher calling in You. Cause them to call upon Your name in good and bad times so that they never forget from where their help comes. Truly, God, Your strength is made perfect in their weakness, and You will give them the meat needed to be sustained on their journey.

God, I pray now that any doubt, uncertainty, or disbelief would be bound up in the name of Jesus and that Your truth will be loosed in the atmosphere. For our unbelief will not make your faith of no effect! God forbid! For it says in your Word in the book of Romans, let **God** be true and let every *man* be a liar! (See Rom. 3:1-4.) For Your Word is a lamp unto our feet and a light unto our path. God, You are holy and there is nothing impossible for You.

In Jesus's name, Amen.

Who Are You?

- The Holy People – Isaiah 62:12
- Sought Out – Isaiah 62:12
- A City Not Forsaken – Isaiah 62:12
- More than a Conqueror – Romans 8:37
- Fearfully and Wonderfully Made – Psalm 139:14
- Crucified with Christ – Galatians 2:20
- Blessed – Ephesians 1:3
- A New Creature in Christ – 2 Corinthians 5:17
- Loved – John 3:16
- God's Workmanship – Ephesians 2:10
- A Son of God – Romans 8:14
- Stress-free – Jeremiah 17:7-8
- The Temple of the Holy Ghost – 1 Corinthians 6:19
- An Heir with Christ – Romans 8:16-17
- An Ambassador of Christ – Ephesians 6:19-20
- Free – Galatians 5:1
- The Righteousness of God in Him – 2 Corinthians 5:21
- The Body of Christ – 1 Corinthians 12:1-27
- The Light of the World – Matthew 5:14-16
- Covered in Prayer by Jesus – Romans 8:26-27
- Born of God – 1 John 4:7
- Victorious – 1 Corinthians 15:57
- Predestined – Romans 8:29-31
- The Branches – John 15:5
- Accepted by God – Romans 8:34-37
- Called – Romans 8:28
- Created in the Image and Likeness of God – Genesis 1:26-27
- Forgiven – Ephesians 4:32
- The Apple of God's Eye – Psalm 17:6-8
- Restored – Matthew 6:33, Joel 2:25 - 26
- Renewed – Isaiah 40:31

Chapter 7
PROVISION

I can tell you about the times I received checks in the mail when money was needed, or when we totaled our car and were able to get another vehicle with no out-of-pocket expenses. Or perhaps I should tell you about that time my son nearly died when he fell asleep while driving. Even the paramedics told him that people don't survive those types of accidents. You wouldn't believe me if I told you that I was a high school dropout who had a baby at the age of sixteen, a second child by the age of nineteen, and was homeless by choice at twenty. What if I told you that I've now been married for over twelve years and have several degrees, including an MBA from a prestigious school.

I can go on and on about the goodness of Jesus the Christ and how He makes a way where there seems to be no way. Even when my guidance counselor in high school said, "You come a dime a dozen," God made certain that her words fell to the ground. As a matter of fact, I didn't even know what that phrase meant, so I thank God those words couldn't penetrate my subconscious. Although others counted me out and underestimated me all my life, God wouldn't let me fail. Hallelujah!

Please trust me when I tell you, "a dime a dozen" wasn't the worst of it. I've been called stupid, dumb, fat, ugly, black, just a woman, uneducated, underprivileged, ghetto, aggressive, and a loser—but God! Had any of those words taken root, I'm not sure I would be standing here today. God provides what you need to make it through your course, and it is totally up to you to grab hold of the tools and the hands that He is outstretching. God provided me with a determination that is out of this world, and I know without question that He is faithful.

Provision

With your gifts and faith fully loaded, allow God to use you how He sees fit. You don't have to worry about your imperfections, your confidence being shaken, or not having all you need. God will provide. He will make a way in the wilderness and will open doors that no man can shut! He will speak when you open your mouth, if you would but believe! If God is truly leading you to a new venture in life to walk out your spiritual calling or to fulfill your passion, know that He will give you what is needed to sustain you.

> "Consider the ravens: for they neither sow nor reap; which neither have storehouse nor barn; and God feedeth them: how much more are ye better than the fowls?" (Luke 12:24).

God doesn't halfway do anything. There is no way that He will give us a mission and not be there for us. Our God never sleeps nor slumbers. He is aware of all things, and He knew when He called us that we were fully equipped. Although we may not see how things are going to work out, take comfort in knowing that it's already been worked out. God did all that He was going to do in the beginning when He created the heavens and the earth. We just need to do our part and walk in the manifestation of God's Word.

This life was never meant for us to wander around aimlessly with no direction. We were always designed to get through life's trials and triumphs with God. Our works will only produce if we are willing to do "the do" and put our hands to the plow. God gives us the power to get wealth, and He will give us the provisions to keep it.

> Who fed thee in the wilderness with manna, which thy fathers knew not, that he might humble thee, and that he might prove thee, to do thee good at thy latter end; and thou say in thine heart, My power and the might of mine hand hath gotten me this wealth. But thou shalt remember the LORD thy God: for it is he that giveth thee power to get wealth, that he may establish his covenant which he sware unto thy fathers, as it is this day. (Deut. 8:16-18)

I cannot tell you how many times I felt incomplete and inadequate. People would often see or tell me about greatness they saw within me, which I could not fully see myself. I always felt that I had a purpose, but I was never quite sure how it would come to fruition or exactly what I should be doing. Over the course of ten years, it was confirmed through many prophets of God that I would be successful, that I would be a business woman and that I would write books. I never imagined that it would take me nearly ten years to catch the revelation. Doubt in how God was going to do it kept me stagnant for nearly seven years. I just couldn't see how anyone would want to listen to me or be interested in anything I was doing, until it finally dawned on me that it wasn't about me. I had to take myself out of it and think about God's greater plan. God uses people to accomplish His will on earth, and I had to accept the fact that God wanted to use me, too. After 100 days of fasting, praying, and reading the Word of God, God allowed me to write my first draft of this book. God amazed me, and He provided what was needed.

"Remember ye not the former things, neither consider the things of old. Behold, I will do anew thing; now it shall spring forth; shall ye not know it? I will even make a way in the wilderness, and rivers in the desert" (Isa. 43:18-19).

God loves you with an everlasting love, and He will never leave you nor forsake you. He wants you to use the power and authority He gave you to do His will. He will be there every step of the way of your journey, even though you will sometimes think He's not. God knows that you will feel inadequate at times, but that is when you have to remember that His strength is made perfect in your weakness.

God asks that we stay humble, stay in His Word, love Him, and remember Him. While you are getting your breakthroughs and speaking to your mountains, always remember the One who gave you the ability to do those things. Never lose sight of how good and gracious God is and that it is only He who gives you the activities of your limbs. It is He who gives time and chance to be successful in our season of life, and only He has breathed the breath of life in us to make all things possible. We cannot miss our chance or opportunity to fulfill our destiny, because we only have one lifetime to make it happen.

"I returned, and saw under the sun, that the race is not to the swift, nor the battle to the strong, neither yet bread to the wise, nor yet riches to men of understanding, nor yet favour to men of skill; but time and chance happeneth to them all" (Eccl. 9:11).

God *is* going to do a new thing in you and it *shall* spring forth! Let the rivers of living water flow out of your belly and allow God to lead you all the way. He is our Captain, our Navigator, our Map, our Guide, and our Life Preserver. He is the Ship and the Sails that Guide the ship. He is the Water that keeps us afloat, and He is the Destination to which we are trying to go. There is nothing impossible for you, if you believe in Him. I challenge you to watch Him perform it in your life, according to the faith that worketh within you!

Scriptures of Empowerment
- Don't be afraid – Deuteronomy 31:6
- God is with you wherever you go – Joshua 1:9
- The desires of your heart – given – Psalm 37:4-5
- I shall not be shaken – Psalm 62:5-8
- No good thing will He withhold – Psalm 84:11
- God chose you – John 15:16
- Whatever you ask in Jesus' name – John 16:23-24
- Don't worry about money – Hebrews 13:5
- Stay humble to be exalted – 1 Peter 5:6-9
- When we please God – 1 John 3:22

Who Are You?
- The Holy People – Isaiah 62:12
- Sought Out – Isaiah 62:12
- A City Not Forsaken – Isaiah 62:12
- More than a Conqueror – Romans 8:37
- Fearfully and Wonderfully Made – Psalm 139:14
- Crucified with Christ – Galatians 2:20
- Blessed – Ephesians 1:3
- A New Creature in Christ – 2 Corinthians 5:17
- Loved – John 3:16
- God's Workmanship – Ephesians 2:10
- A Son of God – Romans 8:14
- Stress-free – Jeremiah 17:7-8
- The Temple of the Holy Ghost – 1 Corinthians 6:19
- An Heir with Christ – Romans 8:16-17
- An Ambassador of Christ – Ephesians 6:19-20

- Free – Galatians 5:1
- The Righteousness of God in Him – 2 Corinthians 5:21
- The Body of Christ – 1 Corinthians 12:1-27
- The Light of the World – Matthew 5:14-16
- Covered in Prayer by Jesus – Romans 8:26-27
- Born of God – 1 John 4:7
- Victorious – 1 Corinthians 15:57
- Predestined – Romans 8:29-31
- The Branches – John 15:5
- Accepted by God – Romans 8:34-37
- Called – Romans 8:28
- Created in the Image and Likeness of God – Genesis 1:26-27
- Forgiven – Ephesians 4:32
- The Apple of God's Eye – Psalm 17:6-8
- Restored – Matthew 6:33, Joel 2:25 - 26
- Renewed – Isaiah 40:31
- Not Alone – Hebrews 13:5
- Fully equipped – Hebrew 13:20-21
- Kept – Deuteronomy 7:9
- Chosen – Ephesians 1:4

Chapter 8
PRODUCING

Most companies are in business to make money, and they want to find ways to do things quicker, cheaper, and more efficiently. They are constantly re-evaluating budgets, the utilization of employee time, the processes used and how they compare to other companies in the same industries. To be the best and to keep up with ever-changing times, they need to always be thinking about the future. They must determine what the organization's short-term and long-term goals are. In essence, unless a company is a monopoly, it must have clarity about what its niche is and how it needs to be positioned to effectively compete amongst its competitors.

Starbucks has become a household name, and people all around the world resonate with it. My daughter, who was only eleven years old when I wrote this book, knows the difference between a Starbucks drink and a drink from one of its competitors. The thing about Starbucks, however, is that the company doesn't only sell coffee—it sells the Starbucks experience. The atmosphere is upbeat yet calming at the same time. As the music plays and people can be seen from wall to wall on their electronic devices, the smells of lattes and fresh coffee brewing invite customers to stay for a while. People line up to give their original order concoctions, as they enjoy free internet and warm fireplaces.

As great as Starbucks is, it still has to focus on improving its efforts. According to an article by Jargon, Starbucks brought in efficiency experts to help baristas make drinks faster. They looked at processes to determine what they could change to become better. Although they had been making coffee for over twenty years, they were still able to increase their productivity.

Just like companies are always finding ways to improve, we need to find ways to advance. People, unlike companies, however, do not need to compare themselves to other people. Each individual person is her very own enterprise, and she is in a class by herself. She competes with no one and only strives to become better than she was the day before.

Are you where you want to be in life? Have you done all you set out to do? Do you know God's will for your life and have you begun doing it? If you are doing God's will, are you still doing it with the same vigor and energy as you once did or has it become an obligation? Are you doing the work of an evangelist, as the Bible notes? Are you feeding the hungry, clothing the naked, and caring for the widow as Jesus commanded? Did you go back to school like you planned? Did you start that business you always wanted to start? Did you write that book that has been lying dormant in your belly? Are there areas in your life that you know are not right, according to the Word of God, and that you know need to be changed?

What will people say about you when you are no longer here? How will your name resonate in the earth? What will your legacy be? If you are not happy with your response, what are you willing to do to change it? Don't spend another day doubting or making excuses about why you can't do what God said you *can* do. Excuses can quickly become lies. Those lies then set up shop and become reality. That reality, sadly, can last for eternity.

"It's easy to be so focused on current production that you don't see the big picture of how productivity could be improved. So approach this challenge with an open mind" (Conerly, 2013).

Producing

You are taking your destiny by storm, and no man can stop your progress! You are gaining clarity about what God wants, you are placing your eyes on the prize and allowing God to do what He does. You have rid yourself of your old way of thinking and have put on the "new" man, as 2 Corinthians speaks of in the Bible. You have made yourself available to be used by God, and beyond a shadow of a doubt, you know that He *is* with you. You are fearless, and the world better look out!

This is a wonderful testimony to have and I pray this is where you are at this point; however, changes like this don't always happen overnight. Some people who have been in church all their lives still don't know what God is calling them to do, but it's okay. This is not to say that it has to or should take years and years for one to get moving in the right direction. Sometimes it just takes reminding and re-convincing to cause our belief in the greater He that is in us to be reignited.

When a seed has been planted, the enemy comes straightaway to pluck it up so that it doesn't take root. Because we are not ignorant of Satan's devices, we have to be aware of any backlash, retaliation, and devils that will most certainly come along to try to place God's people in a state of unbelief, doubt, and procrastination. The enemy would love nothing more than for us to profess that we are too busy, tired, uneducated, or unqualified to do the work of the Lord. He is pleased with the thousands of people who will be joining him in eternal damnation because they refuse to do what God commanded. He wants us to leave the earth being unfulfilled, unaccomplished, and disobedient—but I say not so! It is too late in the game for us to turn back on the testimony of

Jesus Christ. We cannot make excuses about what we can and cannot do because the Bible has given us ample Scripture on all that we *can* do.

Aside from the enemy trying to disrupt your purpose, you may be your very own deterrent. You may be waiting until x, y, and z happen or just being plain old lazy. Trust me, I have been there and done that. It is so easy to get complacent with the everyday comings and goings of life, but that is no excuse for us not being where we should be in God. Time will forever pass us by and then we'll make the excuse that we are too old. Well, all I can say is—age may limit some of our abilities, but it never limits God's. While we have breath and life, we have to give it to God. The Bible talks about what the end result is of slothfulness, and I certainly don't want any of us to reap its benefits.

> "How long wilt thou sleep, O sluggard? when wilt thou arise out of thy sleep? Yet a little sleep, a little slumber, a little folding of the hands to sleep: so shall thy poverty come as one that travelleth, and thy want as an armed man" (Prov. 6:9-11).

I don't think it can be any clearer on what will happen if we do not do what thus saith the Lord! God didn't put us here to take up space. Life wasn't just meant for us to go to work, go to school, watch television, go on trips, chill on the weekends, retire, and one day occupy a grave. We were put on this earth to give God glory with our lives. He put us here to produce. When Jesus comes to collect the fruit that should be produced in our lives, He does not want to come back to an empty tree. The Bible says that God's Word will not return to Him void, but it will accomplish what He pleases. Because we are the spoken Word of God, we must be found doing what God desires.

Can anyone say how many days he/she has left on earth? Does anyone know how his/her situation might change due to the issues of life? Sure, we can say that we'll do it tomorrow, but do we really know that tomorrow will come? We live in a day where the next minute isn't promised! We should not put off or ignore what God is impressing on our hearts. Some things that we are chosen to do will require help from others, whereas some things just require a "yes." The important thing is to start doing something.

Just as God has predestined us to do great and wonderful things, it is also in our power to choose *not* to do them. God is a gentleman, and He will not make us do anything. He gives us a free choice to choose or deny Him. If we chose not to accept Him, the Bible says that He will not accept us. I don't know about you, but I do not want to go through eternity apart from God. God loves us and only wants the best for us. Will being productive in the kingdom of God be challenging and susceptible to obstacles? Of course it will be, but it will not be in vain.

Scriptures on What Every Believer Should Do
- Win souls for Christ – Proverbs 11:30
- Act justly, love mercy, walk humbly – Micah 6:8
- Treat others right – Matthew 7:12
- Preach the gospel – Matthew 16:15
- Make disciples – Matthew 28:19-20
- Love your enemies – Luke 6:27-28
- Be merciful – Luke 6:36
- Be a disciple of Jesus Christ – Luke 9:23
- Be immmovable, steadfast – 1 Corinthians 15:58
- Understand the will of God – Ephesians 5: 15-17
- Be sanctified – 1 Thessalonians 4:3
- Come to the knowledge of truth – 1 Timothy 2:4
- Persevere – Hebrews 10:36

Tilling the Ground
Similar to gardening, one must be sure that her spiritual ground is prepped and prepared to reap a harvest. What is it that you want to

produce? What does God want you to produce? Are you content with where you are in life, or do you have a burning desire within you to do something more? Where do you see yourself in five years? Do you know if you have five years left to live? Where do you start? When do you start? Have you missed your chance? Is it too late? With all the questions that may be conjured up, there is but one end result that should be sought—production!

If you haven't caught on by now, I have been asking the same types of questions and using some of the same scriptures on purpose. As much as I believe you are called to do a great work, I want to be sure that you believe it. Some of us don't get it as quickly as others. It took me years to start doing something with what God showed me, although it didn't have to be that way. I heard a lot of encouraging sermons, I fasted, I prayed and the whole nine yards all without forward movement. What was the problem? What was holding me back? Why didn't it click? The issue was that I did not believe and could not accept the fact that an all-loving God wanted to use me—a sinner. I'm not sure if any of this applies to you, but I have to believe that I am not the only one who has experienced this internal struggle.

In the beginning when God created the heavens and earth, there was not a man to till the ground according to Genesis 2:5. Before Adam, God caused a mist to come out of the ground and water the garden of Eden. When Adam was created, God commanded that he take dominion over the earth and subdue it. According to Genesis 2:15, he was placed in the garden to keep it and dress it. Can you imagine the responsibility Adam had on his hands? Now of course before Adam fell into sin, tilling the ground was easy. In today's world, however, we have to work a lot harder to cause the ground to yield an increase. There will be things that try to choke the very life out of our fruit, but because we have the power of God residing in us, we can overcome every obstacle. Opposition will most definitely come, but we must be steadfast, immovable, persistent, and driven to accomplish what thus saith the Lord!

And unto Adam he said, Because thou hast hearkened unto the voice of thy wife, and hast eaten of the tree, of which I commanded thee, saying, Thou shalt not eat of it: cursed is the ground for thy sake; in sorrow shalt thou eat of it all the days of thy life. Thorns also and thistles shall it bring forth to thee; and thou shalt eat the herb of the field; in the sweat of thy face shalt thou eat bread, till thou return unto the ground; for out of it wast thou taken: for dust thou art, and unto dust shalt thou return (Gen. 3:17-19).

Before the ground can be tilled, one must know what needs to be done. The ground cannot be too wet, too hard, have too many sticks or twigs, or be too cold in order to plant. When the ground is not tilled correctly, it is quite possible that something else will grow in the place of what was expected. According to an article written by Hanna Rhoades, there are several steps that one should follow in order to get a garden prepared to be tilled. The one main point that she makes is that one must know when the right time is to till a garden. Below are the four steps she suggests:

1. Mark out the area where you will be tilling your soil.

2. Start at one end of the marked-out area with your tiller. Much like you would when you are mowing the lawn, go across the soil one row at a time.

3. Slowly make your rows. Do not rush tilling your soil. You will only be tilling the dirt in each row one time.

4. Do not go back over a row. Excessive tilling can compact the soil rather than break it up (Rhoades, 2016).

I get so excited when I see the natural steps of gardening, because it is relevant to what must be done spiritually. God is so smart and He knows exactly what He's doing! Before you start "digging," get direction from God. Find out where you should be operating so that you are effective and not wasting time. Once you find out, start at the beginning of the "marked out area" and do not rush. God knows exactly what He has predestined and where we should be. Be patient and go at the pace that He has released. Do not go back over an area, so that the process is not slowed down or interrupted. Be sure you are moving forward and not dwelling on the past—doing that will cause you to do more work and make your process even harder.

Good Fruit

Do you want the very glory of God produced in your life? Praise is the key! We were designed to give God praise, and the Bible declares that God literally inhabits the praises of His people. In 2 Chronicles 5, there was a demonstration of unified praise by the people that caused the glory of God to fill the house. These people had to have been praising the Lord in spirit and in truth in order to witness the mighty move of God they experienced. In essence, their praise produced the glory of God.

> "Let the people praise thee, O God; let all the people praise thee. Then shall the earth yield her increase; and God, even our own God, shall bless us. God shall bless us; and all the ends of the earth shall fear him" (Ps. 67:5-7).

Now one couldn't go around with his hands lifted all day long, eyes closed, and speaking in tongues because he wouldn't get anything else done. God didn't bless His people with families, careers, ministries, and other things if He didn't intend for them to spend time working in those roles as well. God does, however, require that we pray without ceasing. He wants to be the One you call when you have an issue. He wants to be the One to comfort you when you're down and to strengthen you when you're weak. God wants to be your everything, and He desires your praise.

> "By him therefore let us offer the sacrifice of praise to God continually, that is, the fruit of our lips giving thanks to his name. But to do good and to communicate forget not: for with such sacrifices God is well pleased" (Heb. 13:15-16).

As you go about your days praising, worshipping, and staying connected to God through obedience to His Word, you and others will see signs of His hand on your life. You will feel the very presence of God because He will be a friend that sticks closer than any brother.

Scriptures on Production
- Works seen for the glory of God – Matthew 5:16
- Others seeing your growth – Matthew 7:16-20
- God will bless you with more – Matthew 25:24
- Good soil to produce – Mark 4:3-9
- Fruit that remains – John 15:16
- Fruit unto holiness – Romans 6:20-23
- Perseverance – Galatians 6:9

Be encouraged! You can live the abundant life in Christ according to the power that worketh within you! I speak life into your destiny and command it to perform in the name of Jesus Christ. I curse every evil thought that you have concerning yourself and what the enemy has proclaimed in your life, for truly you are powerful! God did not make a mistake when He created you, and He is for you. I pray that every good work that you do will be to the glory of God. For if God be for you, there is no one that can be against you. You are more than a conqueror and greater than you can ever imagine. God is your buckler, your shield, and a wheel in the middle of a wheel. God is faithful and He will come through for you!

"And whatsoever ye do, do it heartily, as to the Lord, and not unto men; knowing that of the Lord ye shall receive the reward of the inheritance: for ye serve the Lord Christ" (Col. 3:23-24).

Who Are You?

- The Holy People – Isaiah 62:12
- Sought Out – Isaiah 62:12
- A City Not Forsaken – Isaiah 62:12
- More than a Conqueror – Romans 8:37
- Fearfully and Wonderfully Made – Psalm 139:14
- Crucified with Christ – Galatians 2:20
- Blessed – Ephesians 1:3
- A New Creature in Christ – 2 Corinthians 5:17
- Loved – John 3:16
- God's Workmanship – Ephesians 2:10
- A Son of God – Romans 8:14
- Stress-free – Jeremiah 17:7-8
- The Temple of the Holy Ghost – 1 Corinthians 6:19
- An Heir with Christ – Romans 8:16-17
- An Ambassador of Christ – Ephesians 6:19-20
- Free – Galatians 5:1
- The Righteousness of God in Him – 2 Corinthians 5:21
- The Body of Christ – 1 Corinthians 12:1-27
- The Light of the World – Matthew 5:14-16
- Covered in Prayer by Jesus – Romans 8:26-27
- Born of God – 1 John 4:7
- Victorious – 1 Corinthians 15:57
- Predestined – Romans 8:29-31

Producing

- The Branches – John 15:5
- Accepted by God – Romans 8:34-37
- Called – Romans 8:28
- Created in the Image and Likeness of God – Genesis 1:26-27
- Forgiven – Ephesians 4:32
- The Apple of God's Eye – Psalm 17:6-8
- Restored – Matthew 6:33, Joel 2:25 - 26
- Renewed – Isaiah 40:31
- Not Alone – Hebrews 13:5
- Fully Equipped – Hebrew 13:20-21
- Kept - Deuteronomy 7:9
- Chosen – Ephesians 1:4
- Productive – John 15:5
- Fruit Bearing – Matthew 13:22-23

Chapter 9

MANIFESTATION

Revelation 12:11 says, "And they overcame him by the blood of the Lamb, and by the word of their testimony." I thank God for the testimony that I am able to share with you since writing this book and taking my own destiny by force. First and foremost, the book being manifested and in your hands is proof that I did something to move forward in the things that God commanded that I do. It is only because of Him and His provision that I was able to put pen to paper.

Also, by now you know that I had a serious struggle with my weight and eating for a long time before I ever really decided to do something about it. I have lost over sixty pounds, exercise regularly, and have cut down drastically on my eating. Because God got the glory in my situation, I am now qualified to help others who may be suffering or struggling with the same issues. Thank You, Lord!

Furthermore, since I stopped accepting my own excuses, God released me from working a full-time job for someone else and I launched my own business called The Greater In You, LLC. The company's mission is forward advancement of the kingdom of God.

These are just a few manifestations of the power of God moving in my life since God inspired me to write this book. Five years ago, I could have never imagined that I would be here today, but by the grace of God, I'm here. I decided in 2015 that I would not live my life in fear and that I would do whatever God wanted me to do. Since then, God has done a work in me that is almost unexplainable. He redeemed me and placed my feet on solid ground. Though just over a year ago I felt broken beyond repair, God showed me that *He* is the potter and I am the clay. I trust Him with everything within me, and I am going to hold fast to the confession of my faith, in Jesus' name. Amen!

Manifestation

This last and final chapter is dynamic in the sense that it writes itself. This is your story! What have you decided that you will do? Who do you say that you are? Are you in agreement with what has been revealed to you through the Holy Scriptures, through the mouths of the prophets, and through your visions/dreams? What has been your personal experience with God been since you've immersed yourself in His word? Are you willing to take your destiny by force by any means necessary, so that God can get the glory in your sacrifice? Are you now resting in God's abilities and not your own?

I wonder if you have discovered that you are God's choice for whom He laid down His very life so that you could live. Certainly you were reminded or perhaps you discovered for the first time that there is nothing that can separate you from the love of God. Not death, nor life, nor angels, nor principalities, nor powers, nor things present, nor things to come, nor height, nor depth, nor any other creature, shall ever be able to snatch you out of the hand of God. Perhaps you have tapped into the power of God that resides within you and realized that God's strength is made perfect in your weakness.

Of all the things that may have been manifested during this time of confession, self-examination, searching, and revealing, I pray that your desire to have a closer relationship with God was rekindled. I hope that you have sat down and reasoned with God, to see how He could change your life for the better. If you never had a close relationship with God and desire to have one, I pray that you will hearken unto His voice today. Tomorrow is not promised and you cannot wait for the perfect time or situation to accept His call. A simple, "Here I am Lord, use me" will do. He is ready for you to call upon His name while He is near and to seek Him while He may be found.

This is the story of *your* life, and only God truly knows how it will end. There is no "fate," as some say, in which you can release your life and see what happens. There is only destiny, and destiny must be taken by force. God is able to do exceeding, abundantly above all anyone can ever ask, think, imagine, or conjure up in his finite mind. Have no doubt that God's plan is far greater than any other plan on the market. He is a just and loving God, and His benefits are endless. He has placed in you the ability to choose how you will walk out your life from this day forward, and He has given you the power to do something about it.

With every decision, every choice and every action, you are shaping your destiny. I implore you to take every opportunity you have to seek God and do His will while you have the chance. There is no such thing as getting ready to do, there is only doing. "Doing" doesn't just start with a physical action. It begins with a mindset shift, a decision, and a desire to move forward. In this season, don't accept your own lame excuses for why you can't do what God called you to do. Tell yourself that you can do everything God says you can! There is no failure in Christ, only victory!

Be encouraged! God will never call you to a place that He knows you cannot go. He will never give you a task He knows you cannot complete. Sometimes it just takes the understanding that we cannot do anything apart from God and we do, in fact, need Him *every* day. We were not made to fumble through life alone, but with Christ who gives us strength. *You are great*, because of the *greater He* that is within *you*!

Now that you have seen, heard, and read the book—what are *you* going to do about it? Is it just another "good read," or will it propel you into action? God already did His part, now let it be manifested through you! Amen.

Father, I pray that Your perfect will be done in all the people seeking You, learning of You for the first time, being stirred up again and desiring to be used by You even more. I pray that the works of their hands be blessed and that You will reign victoriously in their lives. I pray that You will heal the brokenhearted and comfort those who grieve. I pray that You will remove everything that comes to hinder Your people from moving forward in destiny right now in the name of Jesus. For You are a Mighty Man of War and You are serious about Your children. The enemy has no claim to them and I declare it now in the name of Jesus. They are loosed to perform the greater works that You have left for them to do, and I declare that it will be done in the name of Jesus!

They are the lenders and not the borrowers, and they owe no man anything but to love him. You will provide all they need according to Your riches in glory, as You said in Your Word, and I believe it! They are not consumed by poverty, but blessings will overtake them due to obedience to Your Word. You said that You would open up the windows of heaven and pour out a blessing that they don't have room enough to receive. I pray that You will position and ready Your people to receive the blessings and recognize from whence they came. Do it, oh God, according to Your perfect timing and season of their lives.

I pray that You will continue to move in their lives like never before. Cause them to have an ear to hear what Your Spirit is saying to the church. As they seek You, I pray that their fruit continues to grow and be manifested for the harvest. Let them be bold and courageous, having no fear of men's faces. For in well doing they shall reap, if they faint not. Help them to move forward in all You have commanded them to do on this day.

God, Your Word says that the kingdom of God suffereth violence, and the violent take it by force! Lord, we understand that we are the kingdom of God, who will be persecuted for Your name's sake. We also understand that we do not wrestle against flesh and blood (people), but against the rulers of the darkness of this world and against spiritual wickedness in high places. We will not fight against our brothers and our sisters, but we will stand having our loins girts about with truth. God, You said that we would crush his head and that he indeed is under our feet. God, we stand with our authority and take back everything that the enemy said we could not or should not have! We take back our goals, dreams, visions, plans, ministries, passions, and commissions and we command them to flourish in the mighty name of Jesus Christ! Lord, You said that no weapon formed against us would prosper and we believe it to be so.

Father, forgive us for having been wasters of time, doubters of Your ability, and condemners of ourselves. We will no longer sit back as our years increase and our obedience to You decreases. We will no longer walk around as if You made a mistake in calling us to Yourself. For we were created in Your image and commissioned to do a great work. Truly God, You are perfect in all of Your ways, and we strive to be perfect. You said that a slack hand maketh poor and a diligent hand maketh rich. Lord, we don't want to be naturally rich only, but we desire to be spiritually wealthy.

Let Your kingdom come and Your will be done, that You may be glorified. You have made a way when there was seemingly no way in sight, and we thank You for everything. Manifest Your power in all of us, as we follow You, in Jesus' name! Amen.

Who Are You?

- The Holy People – Isaiah 62:12
- Sought Out – Isaiah 62:12
- A City Not Forsaken – Isaiah 62:12
- More than a Conqueror – Romans 8:37
- Fearfully and Wonderfully Made – Psalm 139:14
- Crucified with Christ – Galatians 2:20
- Blessed – Ephesians 1:3
- A New Creature in Christ – 2 Corinthians 5:17
- Loved – John 3:16
- God's Workmanship – Ephesians 2:10
- A Son of God – Romans 8:14
- Stress-free – Jeremiah 17:7-8
- The Temple of the Holy Ghost – 1 Corinthians 6:19
- An Heir with Christ – Romans 8:16-17
- An Ambassador of Christ – Ephesians 6:19-20
- Free – Galatians 5:1
- The Righteousness of God in Him – 2 Corinthians 5:21
- The Body of Christ – 1 Corinthians 12:1-27
- The Light of the World – Matthew 5:14-16
- Covered in Prayer by Jesus – Romans 8:26-27
- Born of God – 1 John 4:7
- Victorious – 1 Corinthians 15:57
- Predestined – Romans 8:29-31
- The Branches – John 15:5
- Accepted by God – Romans 8:34-37
- Called – Romans 8:28
- Created in the Image and Likeness of God – Genesis 1:26-27
- Forgiven – Ephesians 4:32
- The Apple of God's Eye – Psalm 17:6-8

- Restored – Matthew 6:33, Joel 2:25 - 26
- Renewed – Isaiah 40:31
- Not Alone – Hebrews 13:5
- Fully Equipped – Hebrew 13:20-21
- Kept - Deuteronomy 7:9
- Chosen – Ephesians 1:4
- Productive – John 15:5
- Fruit Bearing – Matthew 13:22-23
- The Manifested Word of God – Genesis 1:26-27

I pray that this book was a help to you in some way for the glory of God. I pray that God will continue to bless you as you make strides in fulfilling your destiny in Jesus' name!

If you are not saved, and would like to be saved this is all you need to do. The Bible says that if you confess with your mouth that Jesus is Lord and believe in your heart that Jesus rose from the dead—you will be saved. (Please see Romans 10:1-13). Also, once you are saved, it is important that you are taught by a Bible teaching preacher, attend a Bible believing church, and assemble yourself amongst other believers in Christ. This will be important so that you continue to stay encouraged on your new walk and so that your belief in Jesus continues to blossom.

Please feel free to share your testimonies on The Greater In You Facebook page to be a blessing to someone else at www.facebook.com/thegreaterinyou. You can also email us at thegreaterinyou@hotmail.com or you can leave a message on our company voicemail at 574-404-7328 (574-40GREAT). For speaking engagements, please send details to thegreaterinyou@hotmail.com. Thank you so much and God bless you!

Other Upcoming Titles
- *Food Is Good, But It's Not Worth Dying For*
- *The Spirit of Power, Love, and a Sound Mind*

- *I Ain't Got Time for This 9 to 5*
- *Purpose Under Pressure*
- *My Inner Fat Girl*

Sources

Conerly, Bill. "How to Increase Production." Posted September 6, 2013. *Forbes. www.forbes.com.* (Accessed December 14, 2016.)

"fasting." *Dictionary.com 2016. www.dictionary.com.* (Accessed January 26, 2016.)

Hunt, T. W., and King, C. W. *In God's Presence.* Nashville: B & H Publishers, 2001.

Jargon, J. "Latest Starbucks Buzzword: 'Lean' Japanese Techniques." Posted August 4, 2009. *The Wall Street Journal. www.wsj.com.* (Accessed December 10, 2016.)

Rhoades, H. "How to Till a Garden: Tilling Your Soil." *Gardening Knowhow 2016. www.gardeningknowhow.com.* (Accessed February 28, 2016.)

ORDER INFORMATION

To order additional copies of this book, please visit
www.redemption-press.com.
Also available on Amazon.com and BarnesandNoble.com
Or by calling toll free 1-844-2REDEEM.

CPSIA information can be obtained
at www.ICGtesting.com
Printed in the USA
FFOW01n0810230417
34819FF